"What place have the Scriptures in the lives of young adults? *The Bible and Digital Millennials* analyses the findings of two surveys of millennials, Christian and otherwise, looking at their faith and interaction with the Scriptures. It is an academic book, that is, it is factual, discursive, and backed up by appropriate references. It shows that millennials are mostly indifferent towards the Bible rather than antagonistic, and some of their actions betray that neutrality. The analysis is helpfully broken down into three groups – Christian, Other Religions, and those with No Religion, and some (under half) in each group do engage with the Bible, mostly when at a church service, and most commonly when it is a printed version rather than in a digital format. There is a built-in tolerance towards religions in the UK, but Christianity isn't a *laissez-faire* religion – its followers are bidden to be productive in taking the gospel into all the world. These survey summaries indicate no room for complacency either on the part of the commissioner of them (Bible Society), nor the agents through whom the Bible is so often transmitted (the church and its clergy), nor the congregational participants, especially if Millennials."

Dr Peter Brierley, Brierley Consultancy, UK

"For those seeking to understand the changing landscape of Christianity in the UK, the attitudes and behaviours of the generation known as millennials are of significant interest. In this study, CODEC draw on survey data of nearly 2000 'digital' millennials to reveal how young adults think about and engage with the Bible in particular. Their clearly written analysis makes this data set accessible and useful, and covers a range of interesting topics including the Bible and social media, and comparison with the US context. This valuable and thought-provoking study will be of interest to sociologists and theologians, as well as missional organisations and church leaders."

Dr Rhiannon McAleer, Head of Research, Bible Society, UK

"I have found this research incredibly helpful. We know the Bible is not an optional extra for Christian faith and discipleship, and yet it has felt increasingly difficult to confidently engage young adults with Scripture. This research helps us navigate the changing landscape of how young adults are accessing the Bible through technology or being distracted by the digital revolution. I have found it revealing to see how unmoved millennials appear to be about the Bible, there seems to be a serious lack of passion and commitment to the importance and power of the Bible to orientate, navigate and transform lives. I hope the church can be challenged and equipped by this research to step up its discipleship around the word of God and bring back the joy and discipline of living lives shaped by Scripture."

Rev Miriam Swaffield, Global Student Mission Leader
for Fusion Movement, UK

"Through this timely book, CODEC's researchers have plugged a large gap in our knowledge of how contemporary Britons engage with the Bible. Data from a robust national survey of digitally-savvy millennials are clearly presented, in non-technical language and figures, and dispassionately analysed. These young adults exhibited a qualified indifference towards the Bible. Meaningful comparisons are drawn with an opportunity sample of predominantly evangelical UK churchgoers and with recent studies among the US population. The work will be essential (and challenging) reading for empirical theologians and church leaders seeking insights into the future reception of the Bible in a digital world."

Dr Clive D. Field, University of Birmingham
and British Religion in Numbers, UK

The Bible and Digital Millennials

The Bible and Digital Millennials explores the place of the Bible in the lives of 18 to 35 year-olds who have been born into the digital age. As the use of digital media becomes increasingly pervasive, it should follow that it will have a significant effect on people's engagement with religion and the sacred texts associated with it. Drawing on contemporary in-depth surveys, this study unpacks digital millennials' stance towards, use of and engagement with the Bible in both offline and online settings.

The book features results from a nationally representative survey of 2,000 young British people specifically commissioned for this project. The data is also compared with the findings of others, including a poll of 850 British Bible-centric Christians and recent Bible engagement surveys from the USA.

This book investigates the relevance of the Bible to the lives of those who have grown up in the digital age. It will, therefore, offer fresh insight to any scholar of biblical studies, religion and digital media, and religious studies.

This book was co-authored by a team from the CODEC Research Centre for Digital Theology, Durham University, UK: **David G. Ford** (Post-Doctoral Research Assistant), **Joshua L. Mann** (Research Fellow for Biblical Literacy) and **Peter M. Phillips** (Research Fellow in Digital Theology and Director of CODEC).

Routledge Focus on Religion

Amoris Laetitia and the Spirit of Vatican II
The Source of Controversy
Mariusz Biliniewicz

Muslim and Jew
Origins, Growth, Resentment
Aaron Hughes

The Bible and Digital Millennials
David G. Ford, Joshua L. Mann and Peter M. Phillips

For more information about this series, please visit: https://www.routledge.com/Routledge-Focus-on-Religion/book-series/RFR

The Bible and Digital Millennials

David G. Ford, Joshua L. Mann
and Peter M. Phillips

LONDON AND NEW YORK

First published 2019
by Routledge
2 Park Square, Milton Park, Abingdon, Oxon OX14 4RN

and by Routledge
605 Third Avenue, New York, NY 10017

First issued in paperback 2021

Routledge is an imprint of the Taylor & Francis Group, an informa business

© 2019 David G. Ford, Joshua L. Mann and Peter M. Phillips

The right of David G. Ford, Joshua L. Mann and Peter M. Phillips
to be identified as authors of this work has been asserted by them in
accordance with sections 77 and 78 of the Copyright, Designs and Patents
Act 1988.

British Library Cataloguing-in-Publication Data
A catalogue record for this book is available from the British Library

Library of Congress Cataloging-in-Publication Data
Names: Ford, David G., author.
Title: The Bible and digital millennials / David G. Ford, Joshua L. Mann,
and Peter M. Phillips.
Description: New York: Routledge, 2019. | Series: Routledge focus on
religion | Includes bibliographical references and index.
Identifiers: LCCN 2018059886 (print) | LCCN 2019005833 (ebook) |
ISBN 9780429435768 (e-book) | ISBN 9780429788970 (PDF) |
ISBN 9780429788963 (ePub) | ISBN 9780429788956 (Mobi) |
ISBN 9781138350687 (hardback : alk. paper)
Subjects: LCSH: Generation Y–Religious life. | Young adults–Religious
life. | Bible. | Digital media. | Christianity and culture.
Classification: LCC BV4529.2 (ebook) | LCC BV4529.2 .F67 2019
(print) | DDC 220.084/2–dc23
LC record available at https://lccn.loc.gov/2018059886

ISBN 13: 978-0-367-78808-7 (pbk)
ISBN 13: 978-1-138-35068-7 (hbk)

Typeset in Times New Roman
by Deanta Global Publishing Services, Chennai, India

Contents

Figures

Tables

Acknowledgements

This book builds on research commissioned by the British and Foreign Bible Society (hereafter called "Bible Society"). Throughout the designing of the digital millennials Bible survey, analysing of the data and writing of this book, Rhiannon McAleer (Head of Research for Bible Society) has acted as a critical friend. Her time, insight and generosity have been greatly appreciated. The research consultancy firm ComRes carried out the large national survey and wrote an initial summary of it, the data generated by them is presented in this book. We are grateful for their professionalism and flexibility. Thanks are also due to Ruth Perrin (research fellow and author of *The Bible Reading of Young Evangelicals*), Brooke Hempell (Barna's SVP for Research) and Edd Phillips (freelance researcher), who gave their time and engaged constructively with the study at key points.

Introduction

Christianity is a diverse religion; it looks different in different places. In the twenty-first century, this is perhaps most clearly seen by the thousands of denominations that span the globe, each with their own nuance or distinct practice (Johnson *et al.*, 2016, p. 26). Part of the reason for this is the degree of plasticity Christianity has, of which the Bible is a good example. What was once communicated orally was then written onto scrolls, and then later codices. The printing press made the mass production of Bibles possible, and the digital revolution has resulted in the proliferation of digital Bibles. Each of these ways of capturing and communicating the biblical content also shapes what is communicated. If someone were to verbally tell a Bible story, the tone of voice and facial expression used would complement and nuance what was being said. The Bible story is being mediated through an individual and the act of storytelling. In the case of a paper Bible, the bookish features (i.e. peritext) mediate the Bible passage that is being read (Genette, 1997, pp. 261–264). These include the single bound volume with a double column layout. In this instance, there are fewer extra textual clues as to how certain words should be interpreted but the book technology being used (i.e. the paper Bible) makes obvious that the text being read is part of a much larger whole.

In light of Christianity's flexibility and the way in which biblical content is always accessed or engaged through a medium, Bible Society commissioned a study exploring the impact of the digital revolution on the Bible. At a popular lay Christian level, the Bible, or part of it, can be engaged via an app on a smartphone; a website on a PC; a children's game on a tablet; a Facebook post that is glanced at; a podcast that is downloaded; or a blog that is read regularly. Much as there are thousands of denominations globally, there are thousands of ways to engage with the Bible through a digital medium. To narrow the study down, the research was focused on the British context and on one cohort of society: digital millennials. They are the first generation to be born into a digital world and understanding their engagement with the Bible was the aim of the study and the subject of this book.

The place of the Bible in the lives of British people

There has been little coordinated or longitudinal research into the place of the Bible in the lives of British people.[1] While a large number of surveys have been carried out over the past 50–60 years, they have tended to be sporadic and limited in nature. Clive Field drew some of these studies together and undertook a meta-analysis with data from 123 national and 35 local and national Bible surveys (2014).[2] This is the most comprehensive work available that traces different elements of British biblical literacy as found in representative surveys and some of its key findings are as follows:

1 "Household ownership of the Bible has slumped" (2014, p. 517). In the 1940s and '50s around 90% of homes had a Bible in them, but a transition is noted and the most recent figures for household ownership are 67% (in 2007) and 52% (in 2010) (p. 505).
2 "Readership of the Bible has declined, with only around one in ten reading it at least weekly and three-quarters less than once a year or never" (p. 517). Field notes that in 1973 16% read it weekly but by 2010 it had fallen to 9% (p. 506).
3 "Knowledge of the content of the Bible […] is decreasing" (p. 517). In 1949 61% could name the authors of the four gospels but by 1999 the figure had decreased to 48%. Correspondingly, 25% of those polled in 1994 were unable to name any of the four authors, and by 2003 this percentage had risen to 45% (p. 508).
4 "Only a small and dwindling minority believes the Bible to be true […] Key storylines in the Bible—Creation, Virgin Birth, gospel miracles, Resurrection—have been progressively rejected as historically inaccurate and/or understood in a figurative sense or disbelieved entirely" (p. 517). In 1960 25% agreed that the New Testament (NT) had divine authority but by 1993 the figure had fallen to 13% (p. 511).

1 This contrasts with the United States, where the American Bible Society commissions Barna to undertake yearly national surveys (e.g. American Bible Society, 2018).
2 Meta-analysis involves bringing together similar surveys undertaken at different times to see if suitable comparisons can be made. For instance, responses to a question on Bible ownership from different surveys in the 1950s, '70s and '90s can be charted onto a single graph (Field, 2014, pp. 504–505).

5 "The Bible has been viewed as increasingly less significant in personal lives and less relevant to the needs of modern society" (p. 518). Field does not provide significant longitudinal data when claiming this but rather highlights recent results (from 2008–2011) showing that around half of adults claimed the Bible had "absolutely no significance in their personal lives" (p. 516).

Field's meta-analysis demonstrates a widespread decline of "Bible-centricism" in Britain. This, he suggests, is a "manifestation of a wider process of secularisation" (p. 520) and corresponds to the related decline in Church membership, Sunday school attendance, belief in a personal God and so on.[3] Peter Phillips engages with Field's work and also undertakes six case studies exploring the place, use and presentation of the Bible across the previous millennia. He concludes that there has been a historical "bell curve of biblical literacy, in which we seem to be in the long tail of decline of the influence of the Bible" (2017, p. 105). Reflecting on present-day British culture, Lloyd Pietersen writes somewhat starkly: "It can no longer be assumed that ordinary people know the contents of the Bible or even the basic outline of the Christian story" (2011, pp. 5–6). All this is evidence demonstrating the Bible's lessening significance in the lives of British people.

However, such a conclusion is not without challenge for others, typically Christians, have found some positive trends among the evidence marshalled by Field. For example, Bible Society's 2014 *Pass It On* report highlighted that 30% of those who do not identify as Christian described Bible stories as being "important to our history and culture" and 29% believed they "provided values for a good life" (2014, p. 19). Similarly, the Christian think tank Theos positively note that 34% of those who identified as "not religious" viewed the Bible as a useful guidebook but not the word of God and 31% thought it was beautiful literature (2012, pp. 21).

Those who have argued most recently against the narrative of decline are involved in the field of contemporary Bible reception. Rather than asking people about their Bible-reading habits and related issues, these scholars have reflected on the use, place and function of the Bible (or biblical images and tropes) in British society (or Western culture). This includes advertising (Edwards, 2012), the music industry (Hooker, 2015), TV programmes (Collins, 2015; Myles, 2015), comedy (Meredith, 2015), politics (Crossley, 2016a), English language (Crystal, 2010) and literature (Blyth, 2015). Yvonne Sherwood coined the term "afterlives" to refer to the continued presence of

---

3 Steve Bruce (2003) provides a brief overview of the decline of Christianity.

the Bible (or particular biblical images or tropes) in a society's culture (2000).[4] Matthew Collins, for example, having reviewed the use of the Bible in the TV programme *Lost*, writes:

> Rumours of the Bible's "loss" to modern society are greatly exaggerated. It may no longer play such an explicitly prominent role in daily life, yet nevertheless continues to saturate our culture and heritage.
>
> (2015, p. 90)

In-depth studies have also highlighted the prominence of particular views of the Bible. Nick Spencer identified three common beliefs about the Bible amongst British non-churchgoers. That it is: a history book; a (fairy) story; or a rulebook (2005, pp. 143–145). This latter finding has been subsequently identified by others as well both in Britain (Le Grys, 2010, p. 132; Theos, 2012, p. 21) and the United States (Beal, 2011, p. 6). In all three instances, the Bible was often dismissed as "unreliable, self-contradictory or malign" (Spencer, 2005, p. 149). Spencer concludes that the only type of acceptable Bible for many was one that made no demands upon the reader and allowed them to pick and choose the passages they wanted (2005, pp. 149–150). Similarly, James Crossley suggests it is a "decaffeinated" non-threatening Bible that saturates British culture, and in particular politics. The image of the Bible held by society and promoted by politicians is one that reinforces Western liberal capitalism; it is a "text of liberty, freedom, democracy, gender equality, and every other thing it is not" (2011, p. 209). Anything in the Bible that does not conform to this, such as threatening people with torture (Matthew 18:21–35), is ignored. He suggests that this is one of the reasons why the Bible "retains its symbolic and nostalgic power" (p. 209).

The place of the Bible in the lives of British people is therefore a contested one. The purpose of this study is not to speak directly to narratives of decline or stability but rather to capture and better understand how one particular subset of society view and engage with the Bible. The focus on one cohort allows for a greater depth of study, and millennials were chosen for they are the first generation to be born into the digital age. To that end, a significant part of this study also considers whether digital innovations, more specifically the use of digital Bibles and seeing Bible verses on social media, are impacting how these young adults think about and engage with the Bible.

---

4 One weakness with research into contemporary Bible reception is that although biblical scholars may recognise an image, or phrase, as coming from the Bible this may not be the case for the general public. For example, "there is nothing new under the sun" is a relatively well-known phrase, however those using it may not be aware of its biblical origin (Crystal, 2010, pp. 5–6).

The digital revolution

The digital revolution generally refers to the technological advances of computing and their impact on society and culture. While it was in the late 1940s and early 1950s that modern computers were first developed, it was not until the 1980s that home computers became mainstream; at that point, computing became *personal*. From the mid-1990s the World Wide Web made computing *connected*, and from the mid-2000s the web made computing *social* and devices *mobile* (Mann, *forthcoming*). Therefore, those in the West born between 1981 and 2000 are the first generational wave to have been brought up in a digital world. They were born at or after the introduction of personal computing and within the age of mobile technology. Some will even struggle to remember a time without smartphones, Facebook and Google. They have been given the label "millennials", "Gen Y" or "digital natives" and are potentially the largest generation in world history.

Generational theory divides societies into twenty-year groups. Millennials are those born between 1981 and 2000, Gen X was born between 1961 and 1980, baby boomers between 1941 and 1960 and so on. These categories are based on broad societal changes rather than subtler differences between individuals or communities, which is one of the weaknesses of this approach. This has resulted in claims that public presentations of these groups are "homogenising and reductive", boiling down a whole section of society into a few values or attitudes, which are attributed to all (Morgan and Idriss, 2012, p. 931). Furthermore, not everyone agrees with the defining attributes given to a particular group. For instance, some have described millennials very negatively, labelling them "generation me" (Twenge, 2014), others though call them "the next great generation" (Howe and Strauss, 2000). Nonetheless, what is typically agreed is that in the West there are certain characteristics and experiences that are reasonably common to this group and have shaped them. These include greater global awareness, a shift towards a therapeutic spirituality, a decline of Christian affiliation and a greater use of digital technology.

Marc Prensky claims the emergence of digital technology is the biggest driver of change for this generation (2001a and 2001b). His conclusions have been challenged (Bennet, Maton and Kervin, 2008) but many scholars still agree that digital technology is a significant influence on this group and their development (Tapscott, 1998; Underwood, 2007; Helsper and Enyon, 2009; Taylor, 2014). More specifically, biblical scholars, sociologists and others are starting to explore the potential impact that digital technology is having on how the Bible is engaged with (Cheong, 2014; Clivaz, 2014; Hutchings, 2015a; Siker, 2017; Weaver, 2017; Bibb, 2017; Phillips, 2018). For example, it has been suggested that reading the Bible (or any book) exclusively from a digital device, such as a smartphone, will result in a more superficial and less memorable reading experience (Siker, 2017, pp. 56–96). Another claim is that the Bible will become unstable in a digital context, with verses no longer being pinned down to a specific literary context. Timothy Beal captures this idea when writing:

> Loosed from its binding in the book, the canon of Scriptures loses its tight closure. Biblical words and phrases are easily liked up with other texts, both biblical and extrabiblical. Individual biblical writings are easily removed from the larger canonical whole to float independently. Smaller snippets of biblical texts are copied, edited, and pasted into new contexts, thereby creating relationships between them and previously unrelated texts. Likewise, other texts can easily find their way into the biblical canon. Interpretations and marginal comments may be inserted.
>
> (2011, p. 190)

Up until this point, in Britain there has been no large study of how those who are at home in the digital world engage with the Bible. There has been research based in other countries, such as the United States (Barna 2016; Goff, Farnsley and Thuesen, 2017; Siker, 2017) or that has used international samples (Hutchings, 2015a), but there has been little work exploring the British context.

The Bible and digital millennials study

A national survey was therefore designed to explore three different aspects of millennials' engagement with the Bible: their stance towards the Bible; engagement with the Bible; and engagement with Bible verses on social media. The first two aspects addressed areas that other surveys have explored in the past, while the final one investigated a uniquely digital phenomenon and has only recently been incorporated into Bible surveys. Earlier studies were helpful in providing a range of questions that could be replicated or adapted. However, in some instances, no previous examples could be found, so new questions were designed, field-tested and used.

The research consultancy firm ComRes was commissioned to carry out the survey and in November 2016 it distributed it online, capturing the opinions and experiences of 2,015 British millennials (aged 18 to 35).[5] Some of these young adults were not as digitally active as might be expected, for instance not owning a digital device. However, the study was specifically interested in how digitality impacts peoples' engagement with the Bible, so

---

5 "British" refers to adults living in England, Scotland, Wales and Northern Ireland.

the sample was refined to focus exclusively on "digital millennials". These are young adults who owned at least one digital device and made use of social media weekly. Of the sample, 96% (*n* = 1,943) fitted these criteria and are the subject of this book. The data presented has been weighted to be nationally representative and has a margin of error of 2.2% at the 95% confidence interval. Much like other surveys, weaknesses associated with this research method apply to the findings, such as people providing what they believe to be more socially acceptable responses. In an attempt to limit this, where possible, data was used from multiple questions to form significant conclusions.

As a sample, 48% did not identify as a member of any religious group, 35% with Christianity, 14% with another religion and 3% chose not to indicate (see Figure 0.1).

The religious labels used above are broad categories and refer to a variety of distinct identities. Lois Lee, for instance, has noted five different ways the descriptor "not religious," is used by people (2014, pp. 470–476). Each group could therefore be further divided. However, to keep the sample size high and the related margin of error low, the Christian group were the only one to be routinely subdivided. In their case, it was divided into churchgoers (who attend church at least monthly) and non-churchgoers (who attend less than monthly) (see Figure 0.2). This was done because the profile of both groups is quite different and in Chapter 4 a Bible-centric group are compared to the churchgoing cohort to highlight their distinctiveness.

Over 500 pages of data tables were produced by the survey; therefore, what follows summarises the key findings from the data, highlights points of interest, and argues for the central finding of qualified indifference. What is presented is valid and accurate, but it is not a systematic representation of the data.

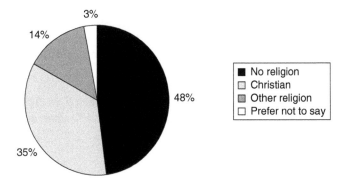

Figure 0.1 Digital millennials' religious identities (*n* = 1,943).

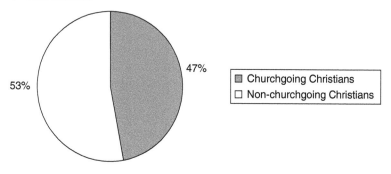

Figure 0.2 Churchgoing and non-churchgoing groups (*n* = 687).

In the following chapters, usually a table or chart provides a breakdown of the relevant data and accompanies any significant discussion. On occasion, there may appear to be a slight error when two or more percentages have been added together. For example, Table 1.5 in Chapter 1 recounts that 71% (*n* = 659) of non-religious digital millennials do not have a relationship with the Bible and 11% (*n* = 98) have a minimal relationship with it. However, 81% (*n* = 757), rather than 82%, is the correct percentage who have little or no relationship with the Bible. This is because we have used the actual number of people the percentage refers to rather than simply added the sum of the percentages (which have been rounded up or down). This occurs throughout the study.

There are also occasions where data is referred to that has not been presented in a table or chart. This is usually the case when subgroups, such as churchgoers or non-churchgoers, are introduced to the discussion. However, full data tables are available from ComRes (www.comresglobal.com).[6] Moreover, due to the volume of data produced some of the findings are not highlighted, especially those that affirm an already established phenomenon. For instance, the uniqueness of London is not discussed. It is a global city and other research has highlighted its higher than average religiosity (Brierley, 2013; Davie, 2015, p. 107–109). In this study that profile was affirmed. Londoners were more likely to:

- Affirm that the Bible should have supreme authority in their lives (31% agree and 35% disagree) than the national average (21% agree and 43% disagree).

6 Data tables were produced both for digital millennials (*n* = 1,943) and millennials (*n* = 2,015).

- Engage with the Bible at least weekly (33%) compared with the population in general (20%).
- Respond positively to seeing a Bible verse on social media (44%) than the national average (32%).

Similarly, the 8% of the sample who identified as "spiritual but not religious" (a total of 16% of the non-religious group) engaged with the Bible more positively than was noted by the non-religious cohort as a whole:

- 23% agreed that the Bible should have supreme authority in their lives, compared with an average of 6% for the non-religious group.
- 19% engaged with the Bible at least weekly compared with 6% of the non-religious group.
- 31% responded positively to seeing a Bible verse on social media compared with 16% of the non-religious group.

This, though, is unsurprising, so not elaborated upon, although the concluding chapter highlights the need for further research into the various non-religious subgroups. What is presented in this book is a central claim and then a series of unexpected findings. These are based upon the data, and they have been drawn out in the hope that others will be stimulated to explore the phenomena in greater depth. A single standalone survey provides a clear snapshot; however, it is not sufficient to produce an unequivocal conclusion. Further research is required to confirm the findings of one study with another or trace the trajectory of the subject under investigation, as Field's meta-analysis mentioned earlier demonstrates. The following chapters outline the findings from this study. They do so aware of its limitations but in the anticipation that they contribute to the on-going discussion of the place of the Bible in wider British society.

Central argument

The study did not set out to test a particular hypothesis or theory, but rather to explore how the Bible is engaged, thought of and responded to by digital millennials. To that end, a variety of questions were asked and an inductive approach was used to analyse the data produced. Over a six-month period, two different teams of researchers analysed the data and the initial results were engaged with critically by other Bible researchers before the conclusions were finalised. The central finding from the study is that digital millennials have a qualified indifference towards the Bible. The majority (50%–60%) are indifferent towards it, rarely engaging with it and having no strong feelings or thoughts about it. However, that indifference needs to be qualified in two ways. First, 25%–35% are positively disposed towards the Bible, engaging with it and viewing it as something of worth. Second, 10–20% are negatively disposed towards it, rarely engaging with it and treating it with caution.

Due to the nature of the study and the corresponding questions asked, not all responses are equally relevant or supportive of the central finding, but most affirm it directly or indirectly. To that end, the subsequent chapters attempt both to present the general findings of the surveys and to argue for our central claim. A number of surprising secondary findings were also noted and they are presented in the coming chapters as well. The three main ones are that:

1   People who identified with a religion other than Christianity were relatively positive about the Bible.
2   Women were not more Bible orientated than men.
3   Traditional Bible formats (e.g. reading from a paper Bible) were more popular than digital Bible formats (e.g. reading the Bible on a smartphone).

These are traced through the majority of the chapters and considered in more depth in the conclusion.

Overview of chapters

Chapters 1, 2 and 3 present the data analysed from the digital millennials survey. The first part of each chapter deals exclusively with the survey results and the second part draws out the main themes and engages with relevant wider literature. Chapter 4 draws on data gathered from a similar survey but made up of churchgoing Bible-centric Christian digital millennials ($n = 873$). The results of this second survey are contrasted with the churchgoing cohort from the main sample. Chapter 5 then presents findings from recent Bible surveys in the United States with which qualified indifference can be compared. Finally, the Conclusion provides a summary of the central arguments and suggests some avenues for further research. Indeed, points of interest and the need for further study are highlighted throughout the chapters.

Chapter 1 considers the data produced by six questions exploring digital millennials' stance towards the Bible, including their beliefs about and feelings towards it. Having done so, the emerging theme of qualified indifference is highlighted and considered in light of other comparable research. The three secondary findings outlined above are also presented.

Chapter 2 recounts how digital millennials use the Bible, outlining their responses to four questions that investigate the frequency and nature of their

Bible engagement. The data affirms our central finding and it is brought into conversation with other studies for it shows a higher degree of Bible engagement than might be expected. This and four other secondary findings are also presented, including the three noted above and also the discrepancy between what people associate with the Bible and their reasons for actually reading it.

Chapter 3 considers the place of the Bible in the social media networks that these young adults are part of. Data is presented from six questions that explore this by asking about their social media Bible engagement and also by providing three examples of online religious/Bible images and capturing their response to them. Qualified indifference is once again noted along with four secondary themes, the same three as in earlier chapters and also the dislike expressed by non-religious people towards a meme that mocked the Bible.

Chapter 4 then presents data from a comparable survey of churchgoing Bible-centric digital millennials. This survey asked the same questions as the main survey but included a further seven exploring the place of the Bible in the lives of these Christians. The findings from this second survey are compared with the churchgoing group in Chapters 1–3 and the lack of social media Bible engagement by the Bible-centric group is specifically considered for it, at first glance, calls into question our main thesis.

Chapter 5 draws upon the findings of recent Bible surveys from the United States. The conclusions of these studies are compared with the qualified indifference noted in the British survey. The differences between British and American Bible engagement are discussed and the reasons for them explored, for they begin to explain why indifference towards the Bible is common in Britain today.

Finally, the Conclusion summarises and traces the development of qualified indifference as noted in Chapters 1–3, along with the three main secondary findings. It considers some of the possible reasons for these findings and ends by pointing towards the need for further research.

This work is an initial inquiry into the place of the Bible in the lives of British young adults. Its size and scope make for a robust study, which provides one of the first glimpses into how the digital revolution is impacting Bible engagement in Britain today.

1 Digital millennials

Their stance towards the Bible

This study of the Bible and digital millennials principally considers three areas: stance, use and social media. This chapter considers how young adults described their feelings, attitudes, beliefs and views about the Bible. These phenomena can be described as someone's "stance" towards the Bible, something akin to their general disposition. While it is relatively common for Bible surveys to explore some of these aspects, such as belief, our approach is broader, understanding there to be many factors that influence how people relate to the Bible. To that end, multiple questions are used to provide a wide variety of data that, when brought together, paints a vivid picture of how digital millennials perceive the Bible.

The body of this chapter outlines the six questions asked in this area and explores the responses of these young adults. At the end, these findings are discussed and brought into conversation with other studies on the place of the Bible in contemporary society or theories of religion. In doing so, we argue that a dominant stance held by digital millennials is one of qualified indifference towards the Bible.

Digital millennials' feelings towards the Bible

Those surveyed were asked how they felt about the six major religions in Britain and their corresponding sacred texts. Specifically, they were asked:

> *How would you describe your feelings towards each of the following religions and sacred texts?*

They were invited to respond using a five-point Likert scale to indicate how positively or negatively they felt towards each. This question purposely considers their affective response, their feelings. Often Bible surveys focus on belief, knowledge or use but not on emotions.

Table 1.1 Feelings towards the six main religions in Britain and their sacred texts

Religion/sacred text	Positive	Neither positive nor negative	Negative	Don't know
Christianity	41%	39%	15%	5%
Bible	38%	40%	16%	6%
Buddhism	38%	42%	11%	8%
Tripitaka	25%	51%	11%	9%
Hinduism	27%	49%	12%	15%
Vedas	21%	52%	12%	13%
Judaism	23%	53%	14%	10%
Torah	23%	52%	13%	12%
Sikhism	23%	53%	12%	14%
Guru Granth Sahib	20%	44%	12%	7%
Islam	21%	44%	29%	8%
Qur'an	19%	51%	28%	18%

(*n* = 1,943).

Digital millennials felt most positive towards the Bible (38%), followed by the Tripitaka (Buddhist sacred text) (25%). Accordingly, Christianity (41%) and Buddhism (38%) were the religions they felt most positive about (see Table 1.1).

However, although approximately 40% of digital millennials felt positive about the Bible and Christianity, a similar number felt neither positive nor negative towards them and approximately 15% had negative feelings. Indeed, for all the other sacred texts listed these young adults were most likely to have neutral feelings (neither positive nor negative): Guru Granth Sahib 44%; Tripitaka 51%; Qur'an 51%; Vedas 52%; and Torah 52% (the data for the corresponding religions were similar).

Thus, at the start of this enquiry, the first picture that emerges is that many digital millennials have neither positive nor negative feelings towards these six sacred texts and their religions. The slight exception is the Bible and Christianity (along with Buddhism), towards which a similar number of people feel positive as have neutral feelings. The reasons for this will be discussed at the end of the chapter, but at present, it is sufficient to highlight the sizeable number of people who responded indifferently (i.e. neither positively nor negatively) to the Bible and all other texts and religions.

While it would be interesting to explore the breakdown of all of this data the purpose of this study is to consider the Bible and digital millennials.[1] To that end, the figure below presents the data for feelings towards the Bible in light of religious identity (see Figure 1.1).

1 The concluding chapter explores a further aspect of this data.

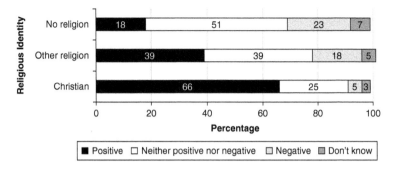

Figure 1.1 Feelings towards the Bible in relation to religious identity (*n* = 1,879)*

* The sample of 1,879 is lower than 1,943 as it excludes the 3% who choose "prefer not to say" when asked about their religious affiliation. In addition to this, not all figures will add up to 100%. This is usually due to the rounding up or down of individual percentages.

This demonstrates that non-religious digital millennials are much more likely to have neutral feelings towards the Bible (51%) than the other groups. Around one in every five of them (23%) feel negative towards the Bible, of all the religions they felt most positive about Buddhism (36%)[2] and the Tripitaka (21%) was viewed as positively as the Bible (18%). Those of a religion other than Christianity were as likely to feel positive (39%) as they were indifferent (39%) towards the Bible, with two in ten (18%) feeling negative towards it. The religions they felt most positive about were Islam (45%) and Christianity (42%), and the two texts were the Qur'an (46%) and the Bible (39%). This in part reflects that 44% of those in the other religion category identified as Muslim (6% of the overall sample). Christians were most likely to feel positive about the Bible (66%) and least likely to feel negative (5%) about it.

Words or phrases associated with the Bible

How someone feels about an object, event or activity is often related to what they associate with it. For that reason, Bible agencies have used word association questions to gain insight into the Bible's "brand" (Barna, 2016, pp. 115–123). With the help of a twenty-word matrix that Bible Society had produced, these digital millennials were provided with a list of twenty-two words or phrases and asked:

Which of the following words or phrases do you most associate with the Bible?

2 20% felt positive towards Christianity.

Those surveyed could choose up to three, ranking them according to how strongly they connected them with the Bible. This format was used in subsequent questions (see Chapters 2 and 4), and the results for the first response and the total for all three often, but not always, mirrored each other. We principally focus on the first response because regular Bible users may have been more likely to provide two or three responses, compared with those who rarely engaged with the Bible. Thus, the top three data may be skewed slightly towards regular Bible readers, and this was something we were unable to quantify.

With reference to the words or phrases that were ranked first, there were two leading responses, the first being "Word of God" and the other "I do not associate any of these words with the Bible" (see Table 1.2).

The popularity of the phrase "Word of God" may reflect Britain's Christian religious heritage and current population where more digital millennials belong to Christianity (34%) than any other religion. What is unclear is whether this phrase has been chosen because the individual believes that the Bible is in some way a divine book or due to the popular use of this phrase within British culture without affirming any sacrality. The popularity of the

Table 1.2 Words associated with the Bible

Phrase	Percentage who ranked the statement first	Percentage who ranked the statement in their top three
Word of God	13%	29%
I do not associate any of these words with the Bible	13%	13%
Myth	9%	22%
Historical	8%	24%
Moral guide	6%	21%
Wisdom	6%	17%
Untrustworthy	5%	15%
God's revelation	5%	14%
Boring	5%	14%
Irrelevant	4%	15%
Sayings	4%	13%
Hopeful	4%	13%
Truth	4%	12%
Inspiring	3%	11%
Challenging	3%	8%
God-breathed	2%	7%
Relevant	2%	6%
Poetry	1%	5%
Daunting	1%	5%
Coherent	1%	3%
Impenetrable	1%	3%
Other	1%	2%

($n = 1,943$).

response "I do not associate any of these words with the Bible" may point towards a view of the Bible not represented in the words provided; however, a varied range were available and only 2% indicated "other". It may reflect a desire not to comply with the survey or something else. It is unclear exactly what people meant by indicating this. The next most popular choice "myth" lends itself to the belief that the Bible is something akin to a fairy tale, and this contrasts "historical", which may indicate a belief in, or awareness of, the Bible retelling a historical narrative.

When exploring the words or phrases people associated with the Bible by religious identity those with no religion and from a religion other than Christianity were most likely to indicate that they did not associate any of the words listed with the Bible. On the other hand, Christians were most likely to choose "Word of God" (see Table 1.3). Significantly, every group link the Bible to the phrase "Word of God", including those with no religion. This raises questions such as: In what way is Word of God an underlying view of the Bible that cuts across religious groups? And why is this the case?

Table 1.3 Most popular words associated with the Bible in relation to religious identity

No religion	Other religion	Christian
I do not associate any of these words with the Bible (16%)	I do not associate any of these words with the Bible (19%)	Word of God (18%)
		Wisdom (10%)
Myth (15%)	Word of God (11%)	Truth (8%)
Word of God (10%)	Moral guide (9%)	Historical (7%)
Historical (9%)	Wisdom (7%)	Moral guide (7%)
Untrustworthy (8%)	Truth (5%)	God's revelation (7%)
Boring (7%)	Historical (5%)	Hopeful (6%)
Irrelevant (7%)	God's revelation (5%)	

(n = 1, 879).

Having earlier clarified that the focus of this (and other questions) is on the first response, in this instance when the data was collated for the top three responses (first, second and third), a different picture emerged.[3] Those who identify with a religion preferred:

• Word of God (24% other religion, 44% Christian)
• Moral guide (20% other religion, 27% Christian)
• Wisdom (20% other religion, 27% Christian)

---

3 The phrase "I do not associate any of these words with the Bible" is not in the top three responses because when it was chosen it was done so singly, whereas all other terms were typically chosen along with one or two others.

Whilst those who did not identify with a religion chose:

- Myth (36%)
- Historical (26%)
- Irrelevant (26%) ("untrustworthy" was fourth with 25%)

The similarity between the Christian and the other religious group provokes the questions: Do the terms that have been chosen typify how sacred texts, in general, are understood by digital millennials? Or are they specific to the Bible? And what are the similarities and differences in how Christians, Muslims, Sikhs, Jews, Hindus and Buddhists understand the Bible to be the Word of God, or a moral guide, or wisdom?

The "myth" and "historical" labels that were highlighted earlier are principally used by those with no religion and this potentially sheds light on the way in which "historical" is being imagined, for it is not Christians who are choosing to use this label but non-religious young adults. What is unclear, however, is what connotations these terms carry for them, which points to the need for further research.

The role of the Bible in the lives of digital millennials

To capture the status that these young adults felt the Bible should have in their lives, a five-point Likert scale was created and they were invited to indicate the degree to which they (dis)agreed with the following statement:

> *The Bible should have supreme authority in guiding my beliefs, views and behaviour.*

This question is similar to many used (Field, 2014, pp. 516–517; Barna, 2016, pp. 17–18) and probes the sense of authority and influence that an individual thinks the Bible should, or should not, have in his or her life.

Around four out of ten (43%) digital millennials disagreed with the statement and two out of ten (21%) agreed with it. A further two out of ten (21%) indicated "don't know" or "not applicable", whilst a final 15% neither agreed nor disagreed with the statement.

Although the earlier question concerning people's feelings about the Bible highlighted a high degree of neutrality (40%), that was not evident in this case (15%). Where in the earlier question 38% felt positive towards the Bible, here only 21% agree that the Bible should have supreme authority in their life. This latter group highlight the positive qualification that is required, for not everyone views or treats the Bible indifferently; some view it very highly.

Breaking the data down into religious groupings highlights that: 60% of those with no religion disagreed that the Bible should be their supreme authority; 30% of those who identify with another religion agree with the

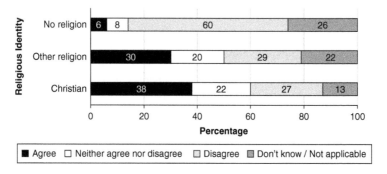

Figure 1.2 The Bible's authority in relation to religious identity (*n* = 1,879).

statement and a similar number disagreeing with it; and 38% of Christians affirm that the Bible should be their supreme authority (see Figure 1.2).

A further comparison with the earlier question about feelings towards the Bible is helpful. While approximately half of all non-religious people (51%) felt neither positive nor negative about the Bible, now a majority (60%) reject the Bible as an authority in their life. This suggests a general indifference towards the Bible as long as it does not impinge upon them, for when it does it is rejected.

It is perhaps surprising that 30% of those from another religion believe that the Bible should be a supreme authority in their life. It seems reasonable to assume that they are not affirming an exclusivity to the Bible which some Christians do (and is implied in the statement). It is more likely it reflects a general valuing of the Bible as a sacred text, or as one that their own religion treats with respect, as is the case for Muslims. The figures for Christians may seem low to some, for just over a third (38%) affirm that the Bible should be a supreme authority in their life. This data, though, reflects the breadth of Christianity that is represented. For example, when the Christian group was subdivided, it was noted that churchgoers were more likely to agree with the statement (61% agree and 18% disagree) and non-churchgoers were more likely to disagree (19% agree and 39% disagree).

Relationship with the Bible

The survey also explored in what way, if any, these young adults thought of themselves as having a relationship with the Bible. A relationship often involves interaction. To that end, this question explores people's stance towards the Bible without focusing only on feelings or beliefs but draws on both along with other elements, such as practice. This question built on the hypothesis that millennials are highly relational, valuing contact with older generations and those beyond their immediate circle of friends (although those making this claim focus on the USA, e.g. Rainer and Rainer, 2011, p. 19). It also ties to literary theories that understand the relationship between the reader and the text to be important (Rosenblatt, 1995). Additionally, the relationship terms used in the question were based on relationship status options on Facebook, the most popular social media platform used by digital millennials. Thus, these young adults were provided with a list of ten relationship descriptors and asked:

> *Which of the following statements, if any, best describe your relationship with the Bible?*

Around six out of every ten (62%) digital millennials had little or no relationship with the Bible. This compares with just over one out of every ten (13%) who described their relationship with the Bible as either "exciting" or "very close" (see Table 1.4).

In light of the majority of these digital millennials not identifying as Christian, it is perhaps not too surprising that 62% indicate they have little or no relationship with the Bible. This ties with later data explored in Chapter 2 showing a similar percentage engage with the Bible once a year or less (61%). In the same vein, where 13% described their relationship with the Bible in very positive terms, 13% also engaged with the Bible a few times a week or more.

A relationship is a connection between at least two objects, and in British society, some objects are spoken of in relational terms more than others. For instance, it is relatively common for someone to speak about their relationship with a work colleague, but it is rare for them to speak about their relationship with their fridge door, even though they may see their fridge door more often than their colleague. Thus, it may be that in responding to

Table 1.4 Relationship with the Bible

Statement	Response
Don't have one	48%
Minimal	14%
It's complicated	7%
Interested – but don't know where to start	7%
Exciting	7%
Very close	6%
Broken	4%
Just beginning	4%
Coming to an end	2%
Other	2%

(*n* = 1,943).

Table 1.5 Most popular type of relationship with the Bible in relation to religious identity

No Religion	Other Religion	Christian
Don't have one (71%)	Don't have one (34%)	Don't have one (22%)
Minimal (11%)	Minimal (18%)	Minimal (17%)
It's complicated (5%)	Exciting (9%)	Exciting (13%)
Broken (4%)	Very close (9%)	Very close (12%)
Interested but don't know where to start (3%)	It's complicated (7%)	Interested but don't know where to start (12%)
	Just beginning (6%)	It's complicated (9%)

(*n* = 1,879).

this question some of those who replied "I don't have a relationship" were expressing the sentiment that the Bible is the type of object that they do not categorise as being relational (much like a fridge door). Whatever the case, many digital millennials have a weak or non-existent relationship with the Bible or view it as an object which they do not think of in relational terms.

When the data was broken down by religious identity, the first and second answers for all three groups were the same: I don't have a relationship with the Bible, and it is minimal. The proportions were different, with 81% of non-religious people, 52% of those with another religion and 38% of Christians responding in this way. It was only by the third choice that those with a sense of religious identity responded more positively than those who identified as not religious (see Table 1.5).

Such a distribution is not surprising, and the Christian profile corresponds with earlier data showing that only 38% of Christians affirmed that the Bible should be a supreme authority in their lives. Indeed, when this group were further subdivided, churchgoers were most likely to describe their relationship as exciting (23%) or very close (20%), while non-churchgoers were more likely to say they did not have a relationship with the Bible (37%) or it was minimal (22%).

What would they ask God about the Bible?

Until now, all the questions used were closed, limiting the type of response available. To provide these digital millennials with an opportunity to express some of their own thoughts, feelings or concerns about the Bible they were asked:

If you could ask God anything about the Bible, what would you ask?

This hypothetical question gave these young adults the opportunity to write an open response of up to 60 characters. It was an indirect approach and provided another lens through which their stance could be appreciated.

Around six in ten digital millennials (58%) did not respond, suggesting that they had no meaningful question to ask (see Table 1.6).

Table 1.6 Questions asked of the Bible

Question/Response	Percentage
No meaningful question asked (e.g. left blank)	58%
Asked about a specific issue related to making sense of the Bible (e.g. "Who wrote the gospels?")	12%
Made a comment about the Bible, God or Christianity (e.g. "God is as realistic as Santa")	11%
Asked a theological/philosophical/religious question about a different subject (e.g. "Why does cancer exist?")	8%
Asked why is it hard to make sense of the Bible (e.g. "Why is it so confusing?")	8%
Asked for help in understanding the Bible (e.g. "What are the most important teachings or messages?")	4%

($n = 1,943$).

It was noted previously that approximately 60% of these young adults had little or no relationship with the Bible. Now, when given the opportunity to ask a question about the Bible a similar number respond by indicating they have no question to ask. It may be that some reject the premise of the question, such as that God exists, so have not engaged with it. However, it may also indicate a general disinterest in the Bible or a belief that they know the Bible's content and consider it uncontroversial. Perhaps the Bible does not, and has not, stimulated them, so when given the opportunity they find they have nothing to ask.

Unlike earlier, the three religious groups were reasonably similar in their responses to this question (see Table 1.7), suggesting that even for Christians the Bible is not as stimulating as might be thought. Furthermore, churchgoing did not make a significant difference to people's lack of response.

Table 1.7 Questions asked of the Bible in relation to religious identity

Question/Response	No Religion	Other Religion	Christian
No "meaningful" question asked	58%	63%	57%
Asked about a specific issue related to making sense of the Bible	13%	9%	11%
Made a comment about the Bible, God or Christianity	13%	13%	13%
Asked a theological/philosophical/religious question about a different subject	8%	6%	5%
Asked why is it hard to make sense of the Bible	6%	4%	4%
Asked for help in understanding the Bible	2%	7%	7%

($n = 1,879$).

The tendency to not ask a meaningful question across the subgroups could lead to the conclusion that many millennials do not think of the Bible as a controversial, stimulating, or provocative book. Rather, they may think of it as a text from which positive teachings, guidance or encouragement can be found, but nothing contentious or polemical. Alternatively, it may be suggested that this question is one few chose to answer because it was an open question and the desire to complete the survey quickly cut across all those taking part. However, other open questions in the survey were completed by at least 85% of the respondents, and a degree of consistency in their lack of engagement would have been expected.

Paper or digital Bible image?

Finally, in light of this study's focus on the impact that digital technology may be having on these young adults' stance towards the Bible, they were asked:

Please look at the following images. Which one are you most drawn to?

Image A

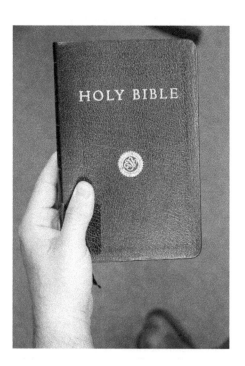

Or Image B

This is a type of branding question, and it captures someone's response to the two images, one of a paper Bible (i.e. a book) and the other a digital one (i.e. on a smartphone). Nearly half (47%) of the digital millennials were drawn to the image of the paper Bible, just over a quarter (28%) preferred the image of the digital Bible, and a final quarter (26%) were drawn to neither.

There was a distinction when exploring the role of religious identity. Christians were twice as likely to prefer the paper Bible image to the digital one (see Figure 1.3). It may be theorised that this is because the paper Bible

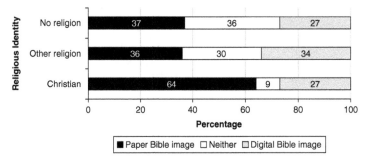

Figure 1.3 Paper/digital Bible image in relation to religious identity (*n* = 1,879).

is an object they are more likely to come across and positively associate with, as they are more likely to attend church and own one themselves. However, within the Christian subgroup, there was no significant difference between churchgoers' and non-churchgoers' responses.

Those who indicated that they preferred either the image of the paper Bible or the digital one were then asked why this was the case and given space to write their response. The main reason why people preferred the image of the paper Bible was because they preferred books (30%), while the main reason people preferred the image of the digital Bible was because it looked nice (37%) (see Tables 1.8 and 1.9). When considering why Christians, in particular, preferred the image of a paper Bible, their responses were similar in order and percentage to those outlined in Table 1.8.

Earlier in the survey when these digital millennials were asked whether they normally read books using print or digital technology (e.g. eReader or tablet), 58% indicated print, 18% digital and 24% used both equally. Therefore, the popularity of the paper Bible image sits well within this wider context where paper technology is normally used for reading. Those who typically read in this way were more likely to choose the image of the paper Bible (50%) than the digital one (23%), and those who normally read using digital technology were as likely to choose the image of the paper Bible (37%) as the digital one (38%). Thus, the type of reading technology commonly used impacted the image preferred.

Table 1.8 Reasons given for preferring the paper Bible image

Reason given	Percentage
I prefer books	30%
(e.g. "I prefer books to e-books")	
A sense of it being more traditional, sacred or personal	22%
(e.g. "This has more authority")	
Physicality of holding a book	14%
(e.g. "Can't beat a book in your hands")	
Aesthetically pleasing	11%
(e.g. "Big and black")	
What I normally use	9%
(e.g. "Used to have one of these when I was a child")	
Easier use/less distracting	5%
(e.g. "Nothing but the word in front of you")	
Can annotate, or flip through it	2%
(e.g. "You can write in it")	
Other response	8%
(e.g. "Hanh")	

($n = 904$).

Table 1.9 Reasons given for preferring the digital Bible image

Reason given	Percentage
Aesthetically pleasing	37%
(e.g. "Brighter than a book")	
Portable and user friendly	22%
(e.g. "The Bible is a lot more portable in this format")	
Adjustable and accessible	15%
(e.g. "Adjustable for me")	
Use their phone a lot and/or enjoy it.	12%
(e.g. "A phone goes with me everywhere")	
Other	15%
(e.g. "Don't know")	

(*n* = 536).

Summary

A varied picture is emerging regarding the stance digital millennials have towards the Bible. Only 16% feel negative towards it, with a larger percentage (40%) having more neutral or positive (38%) feelings. The two phrases with which the Bible was most identified were "Word of God" and "I do not associate any of these words with the Bible". However, it was unclear why they choose these phrases. When asked if they agreed that the Bible should have supreme authority in guiding their lives, 43% disagreed and 21% agreed. The figures for people's relationship with the Bible were starker with 62% indicating they had little or no relationship with the Bible and only 13% describing it in positive language. Similarly, when given the opportunity to ask anything about the Bible 58% had no meaningful question to ask. Finally, when these digital millennials were given an image of a paper and a digital Bible, they preferred the paper one.

The emergence of qualified indifference

These questions were designed to probe various aspects of digital millennials' stance towards the Bible and some of the data presented starts to outline the indifference with which they view the Bible. In particular, note first that:

- Around six out of every ten young adults described themselves as having little or no relationship with the Bible.
- A similar number have no questions to ask about the Bible.
- Around four out of every ten disagree that the Bible should be a supreme authority in their lives.
- Around four out of every ten felt neither positive nor negative about the Bible.

As has been stated, these findings point towards a degree of indifference. With Rebecca Catto, indifference here refers to "a lack of concern and engagement, which is ethically ambivalent" (2017, p. 79).[4] The Bible is a text these young adults do not have a meaningful connection with or strong feelings about.

Other comparable research has highlighted this phenomenon, as can be seen in Field's overview of Bible surveys. What he did not find was a growing antagonism towards the Bible or love for it, but rather that the Bible was becoming less important for individuals and wider society. In other words, people were becoming more indifferent towards the Bible. He writes: "[T]he Bible has been viewed as increasingly less significant in personal lives and less relevant to the needs of modern society" (2014, p. 518). Other recent studies have also noted this. Crossley found that people in Barrow-in-Furness viewed the Bible as irrelevant to much of their lives. Having analysed thirty interviews he notes, "[I]t was clear that there was very little interest in issues of Christianity, the Bible, or religion, or at least very little interest in mentioning anything publicly" (2016b, p. 33). He also recounts undertaking an analysis of Facebook posts from Barrow-in-Furness and their lack of biblical content, highlighting the "baffled responses" to his own Facebook post on the critical study of religion and the Bible (p. 33). Therefore, he concluded that although the then-prime minister (David Cameron) claimed the Bible as an authoritative source, it was one "rarely recognised among the Barrovian sample who saw through his ideological move" (p. 50).

This indifference towards the Bible should be seen as part of a wider indifference towards religion. The first question in the survey demonstrated that in general digital millennials tended not to have strongly positive or negative feelings towards any religion, but rather assumed a more neutral position. In the case of the Bible, this neutrality was rejected only when forced to consider the Bible as a text that should impact their lives. Spencer recounts a similar finding in research published in 2005 that involved interviewing sixty non-churchgoers. He outlines how they described the Bible as having value for certain people or for teaching morals. However, this was only expressed when they had made clear that the Bible had no legitimate claims over their own lives. He concluded that a Bible "which made few (or preferably no) demands on them, was an acceptable Bible" (2005, p. 19). There is therefore a general indifference towards sacred texts, including the Bible, as long as they do not challenge personal autonomy.

4 See Quack and Schuh (2017a) for a larger discussion on definitions of religious indifference.

Nonetheless, digital millennials were more positive about the Bible (and Christianity) than they were about other sacred texts (and religions). This qualifies the initial conclusion of indifference, and although the small positive disposition is not something regularly highlighted, it can be found in other studies. For example, among the surveys that Field analysed, a telephone poll of around 1,000 British adults in 2000 found that 46% identified the Bible from a list of seven publications as having "the most positive influence on life in Britain today" (Ipsos Mori, 2001); an online survey in 2011 found that between 29%–37% of millennials identified the Bible as "important, I don't read it often, but it's got valuable things to say" (ComRes, 2011); and more recently in 2014 an online survey of over 2,000 British adults found that 37% identified the Bible as the most influential book at the moment (Folio Society Survey, 2014). Field notes that there is a general level of acceptance "that the Bible should be taught in schools," something he suggests is because "most adults had first heard or read the Bible when at school themselves" (2014, p. 517). There is perhaps more to this, for the Bible has often been taught in school for ethical or moral debate (Reed *et al.*, 2013). Correspondingly, among British adults, there is also a popular sense that the Bible may have value in the morals that it teaches (Crossley, 2016b, p. 54). For example, a recent YouGov poll of around 1,600 adults found that six of the Ten Commandments were still thought of as important principles to live by (YouGov, 2017). Thus, among digital millennials in general there is a significant but small positive stance towards the Bible that should not be ignored.

This stance is principally held by (churchgoing) Christian millennials, which is unsurprising. However, they are not alone in this. Those who identify with another religion appear more likely to view the Bible positively than negatively. That was certainly the case in this survey where they felt more positive (39%) than negative (18%) towards the Bible and just under a third (30%) agreed that it should be a supreme authority in their life. (A similar number indicated it should not.) Even amongst the non-religious, there is a small but significant group who view the Bible positively, 18% having positive feelings towards it.

This positivity needs to be appreciated along with a negative stance that is also taken by a minority of young adults. These are people who have negative feelings towards the Bible, reject it as an authority and are likely to say they have no relationship with it. This group is principally made up of those who identify as not religious, of whom 23% have negative feelings towards the Bible, 60% indicate that it has no authority in their life, and 82% have little or no relationship with it. Whether this negativity is accompanied by hostility and antagonism is unclear and more research is required into this group. Other surveys have noted this. A Bible Society survey found 27% disagreed with the claim that the Bible is an influence for good in society (Hewitt and Powys-Smith, 2011b, n.p.). ComRes found that 18 to 24 year-olds were three times more likely to describe the Bible as "a dangerous book and should be ignored" (12%) compared with the wider population (4%) (2011).

It may be that people have had bad experiences of religion in general or Christianity more specifically which has resulted in a negative stance towards the Bible (Sherwood, 2012, pp. 9–72). It is perhaps more common that millennials have a greater awareness of global religions and are aware that some use the Bible (and other sacred texts) to affirm morals or values they reject. They may also treat science as the filter through which all religious texts must pass before being accepted, which may result in the Bible becoming not only unimportant but an object of ridicule (Meredith, 2015).

Thus, when considering the stance digital millennials have towards the Bible, we suggest that the term "qualified indifference" captures the survey's findings. These are young adults who have little relationship with the Bible, do not have strong feelings towards it, and when invited to, do not have any meaningful questions to ask about it. However, there is a small subgroup who are positively disposed towards the Bible and a smaller subgroup who are negatively disposed to it.

Secondary themes

There are three themes worth raising and following through the subsequent chapters. They concern other religions, gender, and the digital shift. One of the surprising findings was how positively those of another religion viewed the Bible. In the various questions, they were consistently more positive about the Bible than those who identified as not religious. They were twice as likely to have positive feelings for the Bible (39% other religion, 18% no religion), five times as likely to affirm that the Bible should be a supreme authority in their lives (30% other religion, 6% no religion), and six times as likely to describe their relationship with the Bible as exciting or very close (18% other religion, 3% no religion). Indeed, on occasion, they expressed views that were more positive than non-churchgoing Christians. For example, only 9% of non-churchgoers described their relationship with the Bible as exciting or very close, compared with 18% of people from a religion other than Christianity.

Those of another religion were not overwhelmingly positive. When asked to identify the word they most associate with the Bible, the top response was "I do not associate any of these words" (19%), and around half (52%) have little or no relationship with the Bible. Moreover, they are a small group within the sample (*n* = 267), so there is a greater margin of error associated with their data. Nonetheless, in light of the information available, they were more positively disposed to the Bible than the non-religious group (and the non-churchgoing group to a lesser extent). This relatively positive disposition may be because their religion views the Bible as a holy text due respect; a belief that their religious and moral values overlap with those promoted by the Bible (and Christianity); their religiosity having a pluralistic aspect and consequently valuing the sacred texts and artefacts of other religions; a corporate sense of religious identity and associated value with other religious people because of a presupposed threat from secular culture; being more comfortable with the idea of religion than those who identify as not religious; or viewing the Bible, as part of Christianity (the religion Britain is often identified with), as representing wider religiosity within the public space.[5] In any case, what has been noted is a positive disposition towards the Bible.

In terms of gender, there is a popular understanding that in post-industrial countries, women are more religious than men. Peter Berger, Grace Davie, and Effie Fokas capture the extent of this phenomenon when writing:

> Women are more religious than men. Indeed, for Christians in the West, the difference between men and women with respect to their religious lives has become one of the most pervasive findings in the literature. It shows on almost every indicator (practice, belief, self-identification, private prayer, etc.), and is found in almost every denomination.
>
> (2008, p. 109)

With reference to Bible engagement, Field concluded that "on all measures women are more Bible-centric than men" (2014, p. 518). Therefore, it would be expected that female digital millennials would have a more positive stance towards the Bible than their male counterparts, but this was not the case:

- 10% of women had an exciting or very close relationship with the Bible and 65% had little or no relationship with it, but 14% of men had a very positive relationship with the Bible and 58% had little or none.
- 18% of women agreed with the statement that the Bible should be a supreme authority in their life and 45% disagreed with it; however, 23% of men agreed with the statement and 41% disagreed.
- Women were as likely to identify the Bible as "Word of God" (15%) as not associating any of the words with the Bible (14%), so too men linked the Bible with the phrase "Word of God" (11%) and did not associate any of the words with the Bible (12%).

5 Our thanks to David Heading for some of these suggestions.

There was one instance where women demonstrated a statistically significant positive difference to men and that concerned their feelings towards the Bible: 14% of women felt negative towards the Bible and 18% of men did (40% of women felt positive towards the Bible, more than the 37% of men who did, but this difference was not statistically significant at $p < .05$). This finding will be discussed in subsequent chapters, but for the present, it is sufficient to highlight this unexpected data.

Finally, even though the sample represents digitally orientated millennials, they preferred the image of the paper Bible to the digital one. This may be in part because a paper Bible is a classic western image of a Bible, a book that continues to be sold and used. It could also be because many young adults (58%) principally read from paper books. Recent news headlines have quoted the British Publishers Association as indicating that e-book sales are in decline and have been for the past two years (Campbell, 2018). The digital revolution has not resulted in the rejection of paper books so far, and this has been noted in other research as well. A 2013 survey of 1,420 16–24-year-olds found that 62% preferred buying paper books to e-books. The two main reasons for this were the price of e-books and the physicality of paper books (Bury, 2013; Smith, 2013). The top reason digital millennials gave for the preference of the paper Bible image was "I prefer books". This was the case among all who chose this image ($n = 904$) and was similarly the case among Christians when they were considered in isolation ($n = 434$). This preference for paper books is not a reason commonly given by scholars as they reflect on the differences between paper and digital Bible use. Some scholars have argued that Bible readers are more likely to form emotional bonds with a paper Bible than a digital one (Kukulska-Hulme, 2008, p. 388; Hutchings, 2015, p. 435). They argue that Bible users may have received a paper Bible at a significant occasion, such as a baptism, and may have made use of it for a number of years so that over time they identify it as "their" Bible. Others have suggested that reading a paper Bible leads to a more memorable and in-depth reading experience compared with using a digital device (Weaver, 2017; Siker, 2017, pp. 57–96). They note that the technology itself often influences the type of reading that takes place, with digital technology lending itself more to scanning and skimming compared with paper technology. What the data presented earlier showed, however, was that there are other factors, such as a preference for paper books, which spill over into how people think about the Bible and result in them preferring the image of the paper Bible.

Conclusion

In this study of digital millennials and the Bible, it is suggested that their stance towards the Bible demonstrates a significant degree of indifference. This is perhaps most clearly seen in their lack of relationship with the Bible and the neutral feelings they express towards it. This needs to be qualified, however, because a minority are positively disposed to the Bible and an even smaller minority view it negatively. The various aspects of this qualified indifference have been noted in other studies, although none have given it this label, as far as we know.

This, though, is only one brush stroke of digital millennials and the Bible, and there is the possibility that someone may claim one thing about the Bible but live and act in a way that does not affirm those claims. Therefore, the following chapter explores Bible use, something that will confirm, challenge, or nuance this initial finding.

2 Digital millennials
Their Bible use

Each person has a multitude of pressures that shape their words and actions. Due to the competing nature of these demands, there can be a discrepancy between what someone says and what she or he does. For example, even though someone does not believe in a divine being or higher power, they may, on occasion, pray. With reference to the Bible, just because someone affirms that the Bible should be a supreme authority in their life it does not follow that they will read it on a daily basis. David Ford (2018, pp. 169–203) noted that many of the non-religious men he studied said they did not believe the Bible was a divine or sacred text, yet when they read parts of it they did so as if it were a text of power. This resonates with Michel de Certeau's claim that "each individual is a locus in which an incoherent (and often contradictory) plurality of […] relational determinations interact" (1984, p. xi).

Therefore, despite having reached the conclusion that millennials' disposition to the Bible is one of qualified indifference, this should be held lightly because their actions may demonstrate something different. To that end, this chapter now explores various aspects of their Bible use. This is a complex phenomenon. Engaging with the Bible can be part of an individual's private space of personal reflection: a corporate, liturgical device for worship or a social experience mediated through films, music and art. In light of this diversity, a series of questions were used that begin to capture some of this breadth of Bible engagement. These questions generate a second wave of data through which young adults' use of the Bible is further understood.

Frequency of Bible use

To know how often digital millennials were engaging with the Bible, a broad question was designed that took into account some of the different ways and settings in which the Bible is used. It built on other surveys that focused on

Bible reading or personal Bible engagement (Brierley, 2006, pp. 231–233; Barna, 2015, pp. 94–95), asking:

> *Over the past year, how often have you read, listened to, or otherwise engaged with the Bible, if at all (including during church services and special occasions e.g. weddings and funerals)?*

Around two in every ten (20%) young adults engaged with the Bible weekly or more often, a further one in ten (9%) did so fortnightly or monthly; however, around six in ten (61%) only did so once a year or never (see Table 2.1). These figures correspond well with the working hypothesis of qualified indifference. Indifference would manifest itself in a lack of engagement with the Bible, something seen in the majority of the sample. Nonetheless, there are digital millennials who engage weekly with the Bible, and they make up 20% of the sample, demonstrating the positive qualification earlier stated.

Table 2.1 Bible engagement frequency

Frequency	Percentage
Daily	6%
A few times a week	7%
About once a week	7%
About once a fortnight	4%
About once a month	5%
A few times a year	11%
About once a year	13%
Never	47%

(n = 1,943).

Religious identity made a significant impact on Bible use, with non-religious people being much less likely to engage with the Bible (84% indicated yearly or never) than those with a sense of religious identity. Surprisingly, 31% of those from a religion other than Christianity engage with the Bible weekly, which is comparable with the percentage of Christians (36%) (see Table 2.2).

Among the Christian cohort, churchgoing made a difference with 70% of churchgoers engaging with the Bible weekly and a further 22% doing so fortnightly or monthly. Only 5% of non-churchgoers engaged weekly, and a further 6% did so fortnightly or monthly, levels that are similar to non-religious people. The non-churchgoers were much more likely to engage with the Bible on a yearly basis (50% indicated once or a few times a year), reflecting perhaps their attendance at a Christmas carol or Easter service.

Table 2.2 Bible engagement frequency in relation to religious identity

Frequency	No religion	Other religion	Christian
Daily	2%	11%	9%
A few times a week	2%	11%	13%
About once a week	2%	8%	13%
About once a fortnight	1%	9%	6%
About once a month	2%	7%	7%
A few times a year	7%	7%	17%
About once a year	15%	8%	13%
Never	69%	38%	21%

(n = 1,879).

Reason for Bible use

Bible use is one thing, but motivation for engaging with the Bible is another. In some instances, people's engagement with the Bible can be passive, for instance, attending a wedding at which the Bible is read as part of the service. In others, it may be more active, such as "googling" a Bible passage in the hope of finding comfort. In the former, Bible engagement is indirect and peripheral, but in the latter, it is direct and central. Thus the reason the Bible was engaged is important, so everyone who indicated that they had engaged with the Bible at least once in the past year was asked:

> *You said that you have read, listened to or engaged with the Bible in the last year. Which of the following reasons, if any, explain your reasons for doing this?*

We are not alone in highlighting the significance of this issue; others have sought to capture people's motivations when using the Bible, and their questions were adapted to formulate the one above (Barna, 2016, pp. 59, 105; Hewitt and Powys-Smith, 2011a, p. 49). The participants were provided with fourteen possible reasons for engaging with the Bible from which they could choose up to three, ranking them: first, second and third.

On account of asking this question to only those who had engaged with the Bible at least once in the past year, what follows concerns the experiences and practices of just over half the sample (53%, n = 1,021). This is important because the profile of this group is significantly different to the profile of the original cohort, and Christians are now in the majority. The profile of the group to which the subsequent questions in this chapter were addressed is as follows:

- 52% Christian
- 28% no religion

- 16% other religion
- 4% prefer not to say

To that end, the following data reflects a greater degree of Bible engagement than if it had been generated from the full cohort. The main reason why people principally engaged with the Bible was because it was part of a special church service (17%). This was followed by people not knowing why they had engaged with the Bible (12%) or doing so for comfort (10%) or inspiration (10%) (see Table 2.3).[1]

The first two responses suggest a degree of detachment towards the Bible, for the engagement was indirect and peripheral (such as at a special church service) or unmemorable (indicated by don't know). Nonetheless, around four in ten indicated that their engagement was direct and central (e.g. engaging with the Bible for comfort, inspiration, guidance or direction or because it brings them closer to God). This is a larger number than might be expected in light of our working hypothesis, but it reflects the Christian profile of this sample, and this is addressed towards the end of the chapter.

Religious identity continued to shape people's responses. About half (52%) of those with no religion either engaged with the Bible at a special

Table 2.3 Reason for engaging with the Bible

Reason	Ranked first	Ranked in the top three
I was at a special church service (e.g. wedding, funeral)	17%	28%
Don't know	12%	12%
To comfort me	10%	30%
To inspire me	10%	29%
I was at a regular church service	7%	24%
I feel it brings me closer to God	7%	20%
For general guidance/help	6%	25%
For ethical or moral direction	6%	21%
I enjoy reading it	6%	20%
I think it is an important part of being a Christian	6%	18%
I had to read it for my studies	4%	16%
I had to read it for my job	3%	12%
To prepare for church or para-church activities (e.g. Bible study)	2%	11%
Other	7%	2%

(*n* = 1,021).

1 This chapter continues the practice of mainly focusing on the data provided by the first response.

Table 2.4 Most popular reasons for engaging with the Bible in relation to religious identity

No religion	Other religion	Christian
Special church service (31%)	Don't know (13%)	Special church service (13%)
Don't know (21%)	For comfort (11%)	To inspire me (13%)
For comfort (6%)	I enjoy it (10%)	For comfort (12%)
Regular church service (6%)	To inspire me (10%)	I feel it brings me closer to God (10%)
For general guidance (6%)	Special church service (7%)	Regular church service (9%)
For my studies (6%)	For my job (7%)	It's an important part of being a Christian (9%)
	For general guidance (7%)	
	For ethical direction (7%)	

(*n* = 1,021).

service or did not know why they did so. In the case of those from other religions, their top responses indicated that at least 30% of them engage with the Bible in a more meaningful way, as was also the case for Christians. However, in both cases, the Bible was also engaged with in either unmemorable or indirect and peripheral ways (see Table 2.4).

Unsurprisingly churchgoers were more likely to indicate that they engaged with the Bible for inspiration (15%) or because they felt it brought them closer to God (14%). Non-churchgoers were more likely to indicate it was because they were at a special church service (26%), but comfort was identified as the second most popular reason (13%). Indeed, comfort and engaging with the Bible at a special church service were in the top responses of all three groups outlined in Table 2.4. Their significance can be further seen when considering the data produced by the top three responses, for comfort (30%), attending a special church service (28%) and inspiration (29%) were all popular responses (see Table 2.3).

Place of Bible use

Digital millennials were also asked a similar question concerning the location of their Bible engagement.

> *In which of the following places, if any, have you read, listened to, or otherwise engaged with the Bible over the last year?*

This type of question has been asked in other surveys as well (Barna, 2016, p. x; Hewitt and Powys-Smith, 2011a, p. 47), especially in light of how portable and convenient Bible engagement has become. The participants were provided with a list of ten possible responses from which they could choose up to three, ranking them accordingly.

Their responses to this question should correspond, in part, with their answers to the earlier question about motivation for Bible reading. It would be expected that someone who indicated they engaged with a Bible because they were at a special church service would also indicate that same location as the place where their Bible engagement occurred. However, the most popular places where the Bible was engaged with was at home (25%) and at a special church service (22%) (see Table 2.5).[2]

Table 2.5 Location of Bible engagement

Location	Ranked first	Ranked in the top three
At home	25%	49%
At a special church service (e.g. a wedding or funeral)	22%	48%
At a regular church service (e.g. on a Sunday morning)	12%	40%
Sightseeing in a church/cathedral	8%	34%
At school, college or university	8%	29%
In hospital	8%	20%
On a journey	6%	25%
At someone else's home	5%	26%
At an informal church gathering (e.g. messy church, Alpha or small group)	5%	22%
Other	1%	7%

(*n* = 1,021).

The popularity of engaging with the Bible at home does not appear to sit well with our earlier findings. Nevertheless, while the most popular reason for engaging with the Bible was because the person was at a special church service, it was also noted that around four in every ten young adults from this refined sample engaged with the Bible in a more direct and active way (such as for comfort or inspiration), something that could be done at home. The high levels of Bible engagement at home correspond to the positive strand that has been identified. It also reflects the religious profile of this sample, because when exploring the data by religious identity, it was religious digital millennials who were most likely to engage with the Bible at home (see Table 2.6).

At home and at a special church service were the two places in which at least a third of each group typically engaged with the Bible. Indeed, while a

2 "Don't know" was not an available response for this question.

Table 2.6 Most popular locations of Bible engagement in relation to religious
identity

No religion	Other religion	Christian
Special church service (34%)	At home (21%)	At home (31%)
At home (18%)	Hospital (15%)	Special church service (18%)
School, college or university (9%)	Special church service (12%)	Regular church service (17%)
In hospital (8%)	Sightseeing (12%)	School, college or university (6%)
Sightseeing (8%)	School, college or university (11%)	On a journey (6%)
Informal church gathering (6%)	Regular church service (8%)	Sightseeing (6%)
	Someone else's home (8%)	In hospital (6%)

(*n* = 1,021).

third (34%) of non-religious digital millennials engaged with the Bible at a special church service, nearly a fifth (18%) engaged with it at home, highlighting that although many non-religious people do not actively engage with the Bible, some do, and in their own home.

When exploring the Christian group, churchgoers were most likely to engage with the Bible at home (34%) and then at a regular church service (23%), while non-churchgoers were most likely to engage with the Bible at a special church service (32%) and at home (28%). The popularity of engaging with the Bible at home by these two subgroups, especially the churchgoing one, should not be thought of as an exclusive activity. It is more likely that engaging with the Bible at home is one of a number of ways in which churchgoing Christians engage with the Bible, another being in a regular church context. When taking into account the top three responses, 63% of churchgoers indicated that they engage with the Bible at home and 57% indicated they did so at a regular church service, demonstrating the multisite nature of their Bible engagement.

Bible format used

Not only can the Bible be used for a variety of reasons and in many different places, there are also lots of formats through which it can be engaged. The emergence of digital technology has impacted how people are accessing the Bible, because there are many digital forms of the Bible available nowadays, so the survey asked:

In which of the following formats have you read, listened to, or engaged with the Bible in the last year?

Bible agencies in particular have started exploring the popularity and impact of digital Bible formats (Barna, 2016, p. x; Hewitt and Powys-Smith, 2011a, pp. 45–46), and some of that research was used to provide eleven possible responses from which three could be chosen and ranked accordingly. The most popular format through which the Bible was engaged was reading from a paper Bible, with around two in ten young people (22%) identifying this. However, a similar number (19%) said they did not know which format they had used (see Table 2.7).

Table 2.7 Format of Bible engagement

Format	Ranked first	Ranked in the top three
Read a physical copy of the Bible	22%	44%
Don't know	19%	19%
Listened to someone else in the room read the Bible out loud	14%	38%
Searched for a Bible verse or passage on a laptop or desktop computer	7%	26%
Searched for a Bible verse or passage on a smartphone	7%	25%
Read, watched or listened to the Bible on a laptop or desktop computer	6%	25%
Listened to it or watched the Bible being read on TV or DVD	6%	24%
Read, watched, or listened to the Bible on an eReader/tablet	6%	21%
Read, watched, or listened to the Bible via a smartphone app	6%	20%
Searched for a Bible verse or passage on an eReader/tablet	4%	16%
Other	0%	5%

(n = 1,021).

The breakdown of this data by religious grouping demonstrates that those with no religion were least likely to remember the format used (31% did not know). It also shows that those from other religions were likely to principally engage with the Bible by searching for a Bible verse using a digital device (25%) or reading, listening or watching it on a digital device (22%). Christians were more likely to read a paper copy of the Bible (27%), but searching for a Bible verse (20%) and reading, listening or watching a Bible passage on a digital device (20%) were also popular (see Table 2.8).

While over a quarter of Christians, both churchgoers (26%) and non-churchgoers (27%), principally read from a paper Bible, something that possibly reflects their earlier preference for the image of the paper Bible discussed in Chapter 1, there was a difference in how they engaged with

Table 2.8 Format of Bible engagement in relation to religious identity

Format	No religion	Other religion	Christian
Don't know	31%	17%	13%
Read a physical copy of the Bible	20%	13%	27%
Listened to someone else in the room read the Bible out loud	16%	12%	14%
Searched for a Bible verse or passage on a digital device	13%	25%	20%
Read, watched or listened to the Bible on a digital device	13%	22%	20%
Listened to it or watched the Bible being read on TV or DVD	6%	12%	5%
Other	0%	0%	1%

(*n* = 1,021).

digital Bibles. Churchgoers were nearly twice as likely to engage with the Bible using digital technology compared with non-churchgoers. 24% of churchgoers engaged with the Bible by searching on a digital device, and 25% did so by reading, listening or watching on one. This contrasts 15% of non-churchgoers who searched for a Bible passage on a digital device and 12% who read, listened or watched the Bible on one.

Summary

Just over half (53%) of all digital millennials engaged with the Bible at least once in the past year. For some it was an unmemorable experience, thus the reason "don't know" appears high on certain tables, and for others, it took place within a wider context such as a special church service. For still others, however, it was an active engagement where comfort or inspiration was sought, so the Bible was often engaged with at home.

Qualified indifference

At first glance, some of this data seems to challenge the hypothesis of qualified indifference. For example around four in every ten digital millennials gave a response indicating that their Bible engagement was direct and central (e.g. doing so for comfort, inspiration, guidance and so on), and a quarter engaged with the Bible in their own home. However, these data need to be placed within the context of the wider sample, because those who were asked for further details about their Bible engagement were those who had engaged with the Bible at least once in the past year. Thus the sample size was cut by half and became a Christian-dominant group. If the whole cohort of digital millennials is taken into account, the sense of qualified indifference is more clearly seen. Here are the top five findings for some of these questions, now incorporating the entire sample:

Reasons for Bible engagement:

* 47% did not engage with the Bible in the last year
* 9% did so as part of a special church service
* 7% don't know
* 5% did so for comfort
* 5% did so for inspiration

Location of Bible engagement:

* 47% did not engage with the Bible in the last year
* 13% at home
* 11% at a special church service
* 6% at a regular church service
* 4% sightseeing in a church/cathedral (similar percentage for engaging at school, college or university and in hospital)

Format of Bible engagement:

* 47% did not engage with the Bible in the last year
* 12% read a physical copy of the Bible
* 10% don't know
* 8% listened to someone else read the Bible
* 4% searched for a verse on a desktop or laptop computer (similar percentage for searching on a smartphone)

This more clearly demonstrates that well over half of the sample either did not engage with the Bible in the past year or when they did it was in a passive or unmemorable way. Nonetheless, there was a smaller but sizeable group who did actively engage with the Bible. These practices dovetail with the data about stance towards the Bible explored in Chapter 1 to further confirm and illustrate the qualified indifference with which the Bible is treated.

As with Chapter 1, non-religious people were most likely to be indifferent towards the Bible and could have been negatively disposed to it as well. They were least likely to engage with the Bible, and when they did, it was often as part of a special church service (31%), or it was unmemorable (21%). Christians, and churchgoers in particular, were most likely to actively engage with the Bible and make up a substantial percentage of those positively engaging with it. Those of other religions would also make up a significant part of this group; their digital engagement with the Bible is noteworthy, with just under half (48%) doing so as their main way of engaging with the Bible.

Secondary themes

The levels of Bible engagement found among digital millennials do not wholly correspond to the picture of decline and limited Bible engagement painted by Field. He suggests that among the population in general, weekly Bible reading is about 9% and monthly or more is at 8% (2014, p. 506). Among digital millennials, the percentage found to engage with the Bible at least weekly was 20% with a further 9% engaging at least monthly. Field also suggests that around 77% of the population never read the Bible (pp. 506–507), which contrasts with the 47% of young adults who indicated in our survey that they have not read the Bible in the past year.

It could therefore be that millennials are engaging more with the Bible than older generations. This was something Barna found recently in Scotland. They noted that 11% of 18 to 24 year-olds engaged with the Bible weekly or more often, compared with the population in general (7%) (Barna, 2015, pp. 94–95). A survey of over 4,000 Christians in England also found that millennials were more likely to read or listen to the Bible than some of their older cohorts. For example, 19% of 18 to 34 year-olds said they read/listened to the Bible at least weekly, while only 11% of people aged 55 or over did (ComRes, 2017, p. 11). This data corresponds with others who have explored people's attitudes toward the Bible. A 2011 survey into the influence of the Bible found that 18 to 24 year-olds were nearly twice (14%) as likely to identify the Bible as "a very important book, I read it often and it enriches my life" compared with the population in general (8%) (ComRes, 2011, p. 14).

It may be that some of these other surveys have accurately captured a widespread upturn in Bible engagement among young adults and that this is seen in the higher levels of Bible engagement noted among digital millennials as well. If so, it could give justification to claims that this generation is less cynical towards religion than its predecessors (Davie, 2015, p. 88) and, perhaps due to its global awareness, is more tolerant and accepting of religion in general. Chapter 1 noted that the phrase "Word of God" was popularly linked with the Bible, and this corresponds with the possibility of a warmer reception to the Bible by this generation.

Importantly, the type of question asked heavily influences the responses given. For instance, the 2010 *Bible Engagement in England and Wales* survey found that 7% of 18 to 24 year-olds read the Bible at least weekly and a further 3% at least monthly (Hewitt and Powys-Smith, 2011a, p. 44).

These are considerably lower levels than found among digital millennials but are similar to those presented by Field. One significant difference between the digital millennial data and that generated by Benita Hewitt and Rob Powys-Smith is the wording of the question. The *Bible Engagement in England and Wales* survey asked:

> *How many times in the past year have you personally read, listened to or otherwise engaged with the Bible, if at all (excluding church services)?*

The question used in the digital millennial survey was much broader and asked:

> *Over the past year, how often have you read, listened to, or otherwise engaged with the Bible, if at all (including during church services and special occasions e.g. weddings and funerals)?*

By including personal Bible reading, engaging with the Bible in a church service and on special occasions higher results were generated. Moreover, once survey data are broken down into subgroups, the margins for error increase and that must be borne in mind. In addition to this, some of the surveys referred to above present a mixed picture. For example, the ComRes survey found that 18 to 24 year-olds were least likely to describe the Bible as "an important book. I don't read it that often, but it's got some valuable things to say" (29% did so, which contrasted 46% of the population in general). They were also three times more likely to describe the Bible as "a dangerous book and should be ignored" (12%) compared with the wider population (4%) (2011, p. 14). Finally, not all surveys show this gentle upsurge in Bible engagement among young adults. The *Bible Engagement in England and Wales* survey quoted earlier does not, nor does the digital millennial data when divided between old and young digital millennials. Indeed, Field's meta-analysis concluded there were lower levels of Bible-centricism among the youngest in the population and higher levels among the oldest (2014, p. 518). In this study, however, the lack of a longitudinal component or inclusion of other generations means that such considerations are ones that cannot concretely be addressed by the data. This is discussed further in the conclusion, but for the present, it points towards the need for further research.

Chapter 1 noted that those from religions other than Christianity had a more positive stance towards the Bible than non-religious people. This pattern is also seen in Bible use as well. For instance, those from other religions were five times (11%) more likely to engage with the Bible daily than non-religious people (2%). Those who engaged with the Bible at least once in the past year were twice as likely to do so in an active way (e.g. for comfort (11%) or inspiration (10%)) than their non-religious peers (comfort (6%) and inspiration (4%)). Their principle engagement was at home (21%) or in hospital (15%), contrasting those with no religion who engaged at a special church service (34%) or at home (18%). Finally, they were just under twice as likely to engage with the Bible using a digital device (searching (25%), reading, listening or watching (22%)) than non-religious digital millennials (13% of whom searched, and 13% read, listened or watched using a digital device). Echoing the findings in Chapter 1, at times these young adults engaged with the Bible more (11% daily) than non-churchgoing Christians did (1% daily). In other words, the positive stance of those from religions other than Christianity highlighted in Chapter 1 is not just a passive disposition but is seen in action as well.

The nature of this engagement, however, is hard to see in detail; this is a small group, and the data are not always positive. For example, when asked why they engaged with the Bible and the format they used, the top response was "I don't know" (see Tables 2.4 and 2.8). Therefore, a more in-depth exploration of the place of the Bible in the lives of Buddhist, Hindu, Jewish, Sikh and Muslim young people is required to better understand this phenomenon. It may be that they are making use of a select number of biblical passages, figures or images that cohere with and reinforce their own religious beliefs. Another possibility is that religious people are more aware of religious icons, symbols and material (of whatever faith) than non-religious people. They may be more likely to notice the presence of the Bible in certain parts of British culture and society. For example, a "Gideons" Bible may have been placed in a hospital bedside cabinet, something a religious person is perhaps more likely to pick up and read in the hope that it provides them with comfort or reassurance. Whatever the case, further research is required to explore the place of the Bible in the lives of young adults who identify with religions other than Christianity.

The data considered in Chapter 1 did not show women to be more religious than men, and that continues to be the case with reference to Bible use. Women were less likely to engage with the Bible than men: 15% engaged at least weekly and 67% did so once a year or never, contrasting 24% of men who engaged at least weekly and 55% who did so once a year or never. When women did engage with the Bible, they were more likely to do so because they were at a special church service (22%) than men (13%). Figures for the main location of their Bible engagement confirmed this, with 28% of women indicating that it took place at a special church service compared with 16% of men.

Thus, a consistent and clearer picture is being painted, one that does not show women to be more Bible orientated than men, as anticipated by previous research. This opens the possibility that among this generation, something has changed. The exact nature of this change and the implications of it will be discussed at the end of the book, but for the present, it is important to note that in both stance towards and use of the Bible, the survey data suggest that young women are not more Bible orientated than men.

For these digital millennials, reading from a paper Bible and listening to someone else in the room read it are still the most common formats of engaging with the Bible. In line with the conclusion reached in Chapter 1, there has not been a rejection of paper technology in favour of digital technology when it comes to the Bible. It would appear that at present both formats are significantly engaged and are co-existing. When comparing traditional Bible formats (reading a physical copy and listening to it being read out loud) with digital formats (searching or reading using a digital device):

No religion	36% used traditional formats and 30% digital formats.
Other religion	25% used traditional formats and 48% digital formats.
Christian	41% used traditional formats and 39% digital formats.

This may indicate that the context in which the Bible reading occurs is influencing the Bible format used, such as when the guests at a wedding are invited to listen to someone read 1 Corinthians 13. It could also be that people are choosing to use certain Bible formats in particular contexts, such as a paper Bible when at church and a digital Bible when on a journey. This hybrid approach has been noted among Bible readers in the USA (Weaver, 2017) where there has been an increase in digital Bible engagement but no corresponding decline in paper Bible use. It may also be that some digital millennials are exclusively using paper and others digital. Tim Hutchings found that the digital Bible users he surveyed, most of whom were from Britain or the USA, did so exclusively rarely using a paper Bible (2015a, p. 437). The data available for digital millennials is inconclusive. Even when taking into account the top three choices of Bible format used the degree of hybridity and/or exclusivity is unclear, demonstrating the need for further research.

A longitudinal study would show if digital Bible use will continue to grow in popularity and what impact, if any, this has on paper Bible use. Such research would not only track any developments in Bible engagement but would help explain or theorise, any changes in how people in general, and Christians in particular, understand the nature of the Bible. Joshua Mann has drawn on hermeneutical theories to argue that the physical nature of the text, (i.e. either digital or paper), impacts the meaning of the text (2017; 2018). It can therefore be extrapolated that a shift to digital Bible use will impact how Bible users think of the Bible and understand it.

Finally, this chapter noted that the top reasons given by those who engaged with the Bible at least once in the past year, were:

- I was at a special church service (17%)
- Don't know (12%)
- To comfort me (10%)
- To inspire me (10%)
- I was at a regular church service (7%)
- I feel it brings me closer to God (7%)
- For general guidance/help (6%)
- For ethical or moral direction (6%)
- I enjoy reading it (6%)
- I think it is an important part of being a Christian (6%)

However, in Chapter 1, the top eight words or phrases associated with the Bible by the whole cohort of digital millennials were:

- Word of God (13%)
- I do not associate any of these words with the Bible (13%)
- myth (9%)
- historical (8%)
- moral guide (6%)
- wisdom (6%)
- untrustworthy (5%)
- God's revelation (5%)
- boring (5%)

There is therefore a possible incongruity between why people engage with the Bible—their *use*—and the words commonly associated with the Bible— reflecting their *stance*. Young adults who engage with the Bible are more likely to do so for comfort or inspiration (third and fourth most popular result) than for, say, guidance or moral direction (which were seventh and eighth). Yet, Chapter 1 highlighted the popularity of the terms 'myth', 'historical' and 'moral guide' that are associated with the Bible. In other words, at a general level, it may be that the Bible is more likely to be thought of as, say, a moral guide, but among those who engage with it, it is more likely to be treated as a source of comfort and inspiration. Doubtless, this difference reflects the differing profiles of the two groups, the first having a greater percentage of non-religious people (based on the full sample) and the second a greater percentage of Christians (based on those who have engaged with the Bible yearly or more often). It may reflect the contexts in which many engage with the Bible, such as at a wedding or Christmas carol service where it is usually used as a source of comfort or hope. It may also indicate a therapeutic spiritual engagement with the Bible (Phillips, *forthcoming*). However, it may point to the type of inconsistency mentioned at the start of this chapter. It could be that although people initially think of the Bible as some sort of moral guide, when they choose to engage with it, they are more likely to do so seeking comfort or inspiration. Further research is required to more fully explore this phenomenon.

Conclusion

Chapter 1 argued that digital millennials have a qualified indifferent stance towards the Bible and this chapter has now shown that this disposition coheres with their use of the Bible as well. More than half of these young adults either never engaged with the Bible or did so in a passive or unmemorable way over the past year. This finding was corroborated when further details were analysed. The reason, place and Bible format used all reflect this major lack of engagement. Nonetheless, among some there was a degree of engagement. This was expected from the churchgoing Christians, and in light of Chapter 1's findings, it was also expected in part from those of other religions, further supporting our choice to speak of *qualified* indifference.

Up until this point, the subject of the Bible and digital millennials has been approached through two standard routes, that is stance (affect, belief and so on) and use. However, the digital world has brought with it new ways of communicating, accessing information and undertaking religious rituals. Accordingly, it is important to consider not just the impact that digital technology has on the Bible formats people are using but also the impact of social media on their use and stance towards the Bible. Social media is thought of by some as an essential aspect of modern life, and every digital millennial made use of it weekly. It was therefore important to explore the place of the Bible in this realm as well.

3   Digital millennials

The Bible and social media

This chapter explores data from the third area of investigation: the Bible and social media. The use of social media platforms is a relatively recent phenomenon. Facebook was launched in 2004 around the same time that a number of other platforms were also emerging such as Myspace (2003), Bebo (2005) and Twitter (2006). Some of these platforms have virtually disappeared and others have risen up; presently Facebook is the most popular in Britain (Statistica, 2017). Recent research released by comScore puts the reach of social media platforms at just over 97% among British millennials. Of them, Facebook has the largest reach at about 90% (30% higher than Instagram, Twitter and LinkedIn), with millennials spending on average 25 minutes every day engaging with it (Giorgio, 2016).

Digital millennials consume a lot of information through social media for they browse materials, view adverts (voluntarily or not), read posts and surf timelines. This consumption may be active whereby they are giving their direct attention to the data on their screen, but it can also be passive, such as surfing timelines while watching TV. However, not only is information consumed, but it is also created, and social media use is part of the public self-presentation process to the wider community within social media circles. As such, while consuming can be a private thing, sharing is often public and potentially open to peer scrutiny.

Into this matrix comes the Bible and while figures for the sharing of Bible verses on Facebook are unavailable, in 2016 it was claimed that of the 200 billion tweets sent out, 40 million of them were Bible verses (Lee, 2016). The phenomenon of sharing Bible verses on social media has begun to attract academic attention (Cheong, 2014; Giles, 2016; Siker, 2017, pp. 183–208; Phillips, *forthcoming*) and Christians have shown an interest in harnessing this technology for missional purposes (Drescher and Anderson, 2012; Gould, 2015; Taylor, 2016). A series of questions were designed to help understand the place of the Bible in the social media worlds of these digital millennials.

Frequency of viewing a Bible verse on social media

The practices of sharing and viewing Bible verses on social media are relatively recent phenomena in the same way that reading the Bible using digital technology is. To grasp how widespread these practices are, digital millennials were asked:

Approximately how frequently, if at all, do you see Bible verses shared on social media?

Around half of all digital millennials (48%) never or very infrequently (yearly or less) see a Bible verse shared on social media, and this increases to 57% when including those who indicated: "don't know". Two in every ten digital millennials (20%) see one at least weekly. Thus most of these young adults do not see Bible verses on social media regularly, and this lack of exposure corresponds with the indifference noted in their stance towards, and use of, the Bible. Yet there is a small but significant group who see Bible verses on social media weekly (see Table 3.1).

Table 3.1 Frequency of viewing Bible verses on social media

Frequency	Percentage
Daily	8%
Weekly	13%
Monthly	13%
Once every six months	9%
Once a year or less often	10%
Don't know	9%
Never	39%

(*n* = 1,943).

When the data was subdivided by religious identity there were similarities with the Bible engagement data considered in Chapter 2. Non-religious digital millennials were least likely to see a Bible verse on social media and those from another religion were as likely as Christians to see one (see Table 3.2).

This suggests that there may be something of a filter bubble, where those who identify with a religion were more likely to see Bible verses on social media than their non-religious peers. Religious young adults were:

• six times more likely to see a bible verse daily
• twice as likely to see a bible verse weekly
• twice as likely to see a Bible verse monthly

There is little difference between Christians and those of other religions, which may indicate that religious identity in a broad sense, rather than

Table 3.2 Frequency of viewing Bible verses on social media in relation to religious identity

Frequency	No religion	Other religion	Christian
Daily	2%	13%	13%
Weekly	8%	17%	18%
Monthly	9%	17%	17%
Once every six months	8%	12%	9%
Once a year or less often	11%	7%	10%
Don't know	9%	8%	8%
Never	52%	25%	25%

(*n* = 1,879).

affiliation to a particular religion is the significant factor. However, there was a significant difference between churchgoers who were approximately four times more likely to see a Bible verse on social media at least weekly (25% daily, 28% weekly) than non-churchgoers (2% daily, 10% weekly). This indicates that there is a micro-bubble, with churchgoing Christians being most likely to see Bible verses on social media.

It is unclear the extent to which these bubbles are a result of religious people (and churchgoers in particular) being part of homogenous online communities where the sharing of Bible verses by members is relatively common (i.e. an echo chamber). It could also be that Christian organisations, such as a church or Bible agency, are posting Bible verses online and the people most likely to be part of their network are religiously orientated. Finally, it may be that the algorithms used by social media companies are driving Bible verses towards people who are more likely to respond positively to them. In all probability, a combination of factors will result in some people being more likely to see Bible verses, and further research is required to unpick the interweaving nature that results in the creation of these bubbles.

Social media platform most frequently used

There are a wide variety of social media platforms, and it is suggested that certain platforms are more suited to certain tasks. For example, Pauline Cheong highlight's Twitter's format, one involving writing short texts of no longer than 140 characters (at that time) to which links can be attached, which are then shared with other people who can respond. She notes the popularity of sharing Bible verses on Twitter, arguing that the format is particularly suited to this task (2014, pp. 2–3). It has also been noted that certain social media platforms are more likely to be used by certain groups, for instance of all generational groups, those under the age of 18 (Gen Z) are the ones most likely to use SnapChat (Statistica, 2017). Therefore all the respondents who indicated that they see Bible verses on social media monthly or more often (*n* = 651) were asked:[1]

> *Which social media platform do you typically see Bible verses shared on? (Choose as many as required)*

Contrasting Cheong's focus on Twitter, Facebook was the social media platform these young adults were most likely to see Bible verses on (see Table 3.3). This corresponds both with other contemporary research (Giorgio, 2016) and an earlier finding from our survey showing Facebook to be the most popular social media platform used by digital millennials (83%), followed by YouTube (73%), Instagram (49%), Twitter (45%) and Snapchat (35%).[2] The act of seeing Bible verses shared on Facebook demonstrates the ease with which some Christians incorporate popular technological developments into their religious practice.

The lack of Bible verses being seen on YouTube or Snapchat compared with Facebook or Instagram suggests some social media platforms are more suited to the sharing of Bible verses than others and there may be other factors as well. One is the geographical context. In London, the percentage that viewed Bible verses on Instagram (48%) and Twitter (42%) were 15% higher than the national average. This corresponded with a

Table 3.3 Social media platform Bible verses were viewed on

Top nine social media platform on which Bible verses are viewed	Percentage
Facebook	72%
Instagram	31%
Twitter	28%
YouTube	27%
Google+	16%
Snapchat	11%
Pinterest	8%
Vine	4%
Flickr	3%

(*n* = 651).

1 51% of this subgroup were Christian; 27% were not religious and 19% identified with another religion.
2 Christian digital millennials were no more likely to use Facebook than non-religious young adults.

10%–15% higher than average use of Instagram (64%) and Twitter (56%) in London. Another factor is religion. Proportionally, twice as many young adults from a religion other than Christianity (49%) saw Bible verses on YouTube than Christians (27%), even though they were no more likely to use YouTube in general. In both cases, geographical location and religious identity are groupings that probably mask more meaningful factors. London is a global city and home to people from around the world. They bring with them social media preferences that may be different to those held by white British people. For instance, in some countries such as India and Saudi Arabia, YouTube is as, if not more, popular than Facebook (Statistica, 2018a, 2018b). Further research is required to more clearly draw out the influencing factors shaping the social media platforms people view Bible verses on.

Reaction to viewing a Bible verse on social media

It would be incorrect to assume that just because someone sees a Bible verse on social media, they affirm it. In much the same way that Bible engagement data needs to be appreciated in light of why people engaged with the Bible, so too the viewing of Bible verses on social media needs to be appreciated in light of how people react to seeing such a text (Barna, 2016, p. 121). A series of questions were asked exploring digital millennials' reactions to seeing Bible verses on social media. The first was addressed to the entire sample:

> *When you see a Bible verse shared on social media, what is your typical reaction?*

About a quarter (28%) ignored the Bible verse, another quarter had never seen one (24%),[3] a third (32%) reacted positively (feel inspired, encouraged or comforted), and 13% responded negatively (feel irritated or uncomfortable) (see Table 3.4).

The quarter who choose to ignore the Bible verse are probably uninterested in it, as could be the quarter who have never seen a Bible verse on social media. In their case, the likelihood is that Bible verses are of no interest to them or their circle of friends, and this is the reason why they never seen one. The third who responded positively highlight the presence

---

3   In this question, 24% indicated they have never seen a Bible verse on social media; however, in an earlier question in this chapter 39% claimed never to have seen a Bible verse on social media. The difference between these responses is probably due to the type of question asked, the earlier one asked about frequency directly and this present one did so indirectly.

Table 3.4 Reaction to seeing a Bible verse on social media

Reaction to seeing a Bible verse on social media	Percentage
I ignore it	28%
I have never seen a Bible verse shared on social media	24%
I feel inspired	11%
I feel encouraged	10%
I feel comforted	10%
I feel irritated	8%
I feel uncomfortable	5%
Other	3%

(*n* = 1,943).

of those who value the Bible (or the presence of Bible verses online). The 13% who found it irritating or made them feel uncomfortable highlight that for some seeing Bible verses on social media is negative.

As might be expected, religious identity impacted people's reaction to seeing Bible verses on social media. The majority of non-religious digital millennials (69%) had either not seen a Bible verse shared on social media, or if they had, they ignored it, while most Christians (56%) had seen one and reacted positively. Those of another religion were as likely not to see one or to ignore it (42%) as to see it and respond positively (39%). A smaller group of non-religious young adults (16%) and those from other religions (16%) reacted negatively to seeing Bible verses, and there were some Christians for whom it was negative as well (7%) (see Figure 3.1).

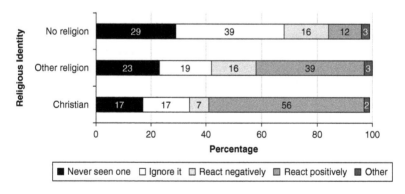

Figure 3.1 Reaction to seeing a Bible verse on social media in relation to religious identity (*n* = 1,879).

Therefore, digital millennials who identify with a religion are more likely to respond positively towards a Bible verse on social media than their non-religious peers. This dovetails with the findings noted earlier in the chapter that religious adults were also more likely to see Bible verses on social media. Significantly, however, a difference is now noted between the Christian and the other religion cohorts, with the former reacting more positively to these verses than the latter. When breaking down the Christian data further, churchgoers were found to be twice as likely to respond positively to Bible verses shared on social media (78%) than non-churchgoers (37%) who were more likely to have never seen or ignored the Bible verse (53%).

Therefore religious digital millennials are proportionally more likely to see a Bible verse shared on social media than their non-religious peers, and this is especially the case for churchgoers. These groups are also more likely to react positively to the viewing of Bible verses. This corresponds well with the suggestion that there is something of a filter bubble where the viewing of Bible verses principally occurs among religious people and especially churchgoers.

Opinion on sharing Bible verses online

The second question concerning people's reactions to the sharing of Bible verses took a different approach. In this instance, the focus was on the participants who in the preceding question had indicated that they had seen a Bible verse shared on social media at least once in their lifetime ($n = 1,475$). This subgroup had proportionally slightly fewer non-religious people (45%), a similar percentage of those from another religion (14%) and who preferred not to say (3%), but slightly more Christians (39%), with a greater percentage of churchgoers (54%) than non-churchgoers (46%). It is therefore a slightly more churchgoing Christian cohort than the whole sample and the data produced should be considered in light of that.

This subgroup was provided with six pairs of statements concerning Bible verses on social media and asked:

> *In each pair, please select the statement which best reflects your view.*

From the six pairs of statements the three that were most strongly affirmed were (see Table 3.5):

- Seeing Bible verses shared on social media does not make me want to find out more about Christianity (52%).
- I do not generally think that Bible verses shared on social media are relevant to me (51%).
- I do not pay any attention to Bible verses shared on social media (46%).

Table 3.5 Response to sharing Bible verses on social media

Percentage for statement A	Percentage for statement B	Don't know
23% Seeing Bible verses shared on social media makes me want to find out more about Christianity	52% Seeing Bible verses share on social media does not make me want to find out more about Christianity	24%
26% I generally think that Bible verses shared on social media are relevant to me	51% I do not generally think that Bible verses shared on social media are relevant to me	24%
32% Bible verses shared on social media usually catch my eye	46% I do not pay any attention to Bible verses shared on social media	23%
41% I think it's a positive thing for people to share Bible verses	24% I think it's a negative thing for people to share Bible verses	35%
34% I think people who share Bible verses are doing it in the best interest of others	39% I think people who share Bible verses are doing it in the best interests of themselves	27%
29% I am grateful that Bible verses have been shared on social media	33% I am concerned that some people may be offended by Bible verses being shared on social media	39%

(n = 1,475).

So even though there are proportionally more churchgoing Christians in this sample, around half do not think that Bible verses shared on social media are relevant to them and a similar number do not pay any attention to them. This suggests that their engagement with these Bible verses is of a passive nature and this sits well with the findings highlighted earlier. Nonetheless, four in ten (41%) think it is a positive thing for people to share Bible verses, and around three in ten (29%) say they are "grateful that Bible verses have been shared on social media". Finally, around a quarter think it is a negative thing when people share Bible verses on social media (24%).

The second and fourth statements in Table 3.5 clearly delineate the sense of qualified indifference and are presented in light of their religious subgroups in Figures 3.2 and 3.3.

Approximately three quarters (73%) of non-religious young adults who have seen a Bible verse at least once in their lifetime describe it as being irrelevant, which points towards indifference. The data for those of religions

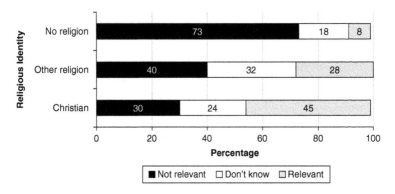

Figure 3.2 Relevance of Bible verse shared in relation to religious identity (*n* = 1,431).

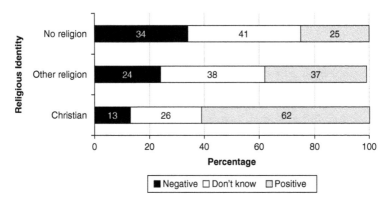

Figure 3.3 Negative/positive to share Bible verses in relation to religious identity (*n* = 1,431).

other than Christianity are more moderate but continue to demonstrate a degree of indifference, with 40% describing Bible verses on social media as irrelevant.

Just under half (45%) of Christians find the Bible verses personally relevant, and more than half (62%) think it is a good idea for Bible verses to be shared. This suggests that even some of those Christians who do not find Bible verses relevant value the practice of sharing them. The positive qualification is also seen among those from another religion but to a lesser degree, a quarter (28%) of them finding the Bible verses relevant and a third (37%) saying it is a positive thing to share them (as do 25% of non-religious young adults).

Finally, around a third of non-religious digital millennials find the sharing of Bible verses to be a negative thing (34%). This suggests that for some there is more than just indifference; there may be an active dislike, irritation or concern. They are not alone in this: 24% of those from another religion and 13% of Christians also thought that sharing Bible verses on social media was a negative practice.

Reaction to three online images

The third question exploring digital millennials' reactions to seeing Bible verses on social media had two parts. The first explored their emotional reaction to three images they might see on social media and the second their practical response to those images.

Three images were presented to the whole sample (*n* = 1,943). These images were:

Image 1—Bible Verse

This consisted of a turquoise underwater scene with a yellow leaf floating in the middle of the water,[4] and a Bible verse placed in the corner. It reads: "A new command I give you: Love one another" and is identified as a quote from Jesus (John 13:34).

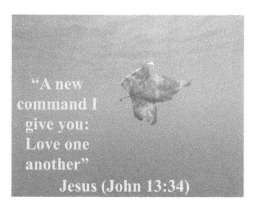

Image 2—Laughing Man

This comprised a picture of a man holding a Bible and laughing at a contradiction in it. The superimposed text "Genesis 32:30 I have seen the face of God" is printed at the top of the image and "John 1:18 & 1 John 4:12 nobody has seen the face of God" occurs at the bottom.[5]

---

4 This picture was accessed from https://unsplash.com/photos/GAoiMKfflZ4. The biblical text was superimposed upon it, as was the quote from Gandhi in Image 3.
5 This meme was accessed from https://me.me/i/genesis-32-30-i-have-seen-the-face-of-god-bible-15280105

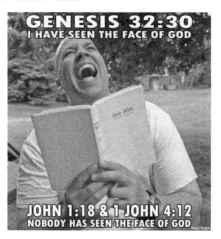

Image 3—Gandhi Quote

This had the same background as the Bible verse image (turquoise water), except in this instance a quote attributed to Gandhi was placed in the corner: "Be the change you wish to see in the world".

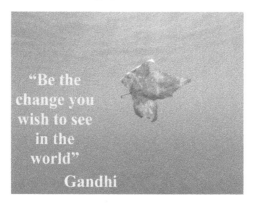

The Bible verse and quote from Gandhi were considered by us to be inoffensive and upholding values that many would affirm. Both Jesus and Gandhi are often considered to be good men who are identified as moral teachers, and both texts were a gentle call to action. The "laughing man" image provided a further contrast by mocking the Bible.

Digital millennials were asked to indicate on an eleven point Likert scale the extent to which:

- They liked—disliked each image.
- How comfortable—uncomfortable they felt about them.
- How engaging—boring they found them.

Of the three images, image 3 (Gandhi quote) was best received, with people most likely to respond positively to it. Image 1 (Bible verse) was received reasonably well: people were likely to respond positively or indifferently (neither positively nor negatively) towards it. Finally, image 2 (the laughing man) was least well received, with people most likely to respond indifferently or negatively towards it (see Table 3.6).

While the text and the image cannot be separated, and there will have been those who found the image distasteful or boring but not the words (and vice versa), nonetheless, how people respond to these images can act as a general guide to how Bible verses are received on social media.

With reference to all three images at least one-third of responses indicated a high degree of neutrality, for example, neither liking nor disliking the image. This proportion echoes that which was seen in Chapter 1 where 40%–50% adopted a similar position regarding the six major religions in Britain and their sacred texts.

In general, the Gandhi quote was preferred to the Bible verse, even though as Chapter 1 indicated, Christianity was thought of more positively (41%) than Hinduism (27%) and the Bible (38%) than the Vedas (21%). There are a number of possible reasons for this. It could be that the sentiment "be the change you wish to see in the world" resonates more with the positive global aspirations of millennials than "a new command I give you: Love one another". It could also be that these young adults are drawn more towards Gandhi than Jesus. The popular persona of Gandhi is not exclusively constructed from his religiosity but rather is made up of a host of attributes including courage and humility. The identity of Jesus, however, is much more closely linked with religion and Christianity in particular.

Table 3.6 Reaction to the three images

Image 3—Gandhi Quote		
Like (54%)	Neither like nor dislike (34%)	Dislike (13%)
Comfortable (55%)	Neither comfortable nor uncomfortable (32%)	Uncomfortable (13%)
Engaging (48%)	Neither engaging nor boring (34%)	Boring (18%)
Image 1—Bible Verse		
Like (38%)	Neither like nor dislike it (42%)	Dislike (20%)
Comfortable (44%)	Neither comfortable nor uncomfortable (40%)	Uncomfortable (16%)
Engaging (36%)	Neither engaging nor boring (39%)	Boring (25%)
Image 2—Laughing Man		
Like (23%)	Neither like nor dislike (38%)	Dislike (39%)
Comfortable (22%)	Neither comfortable nor uncomfortable (44%)	Uncomfortable (34%)
Engaging (25%)	Neither engaging nor boring (38%)	Boring (36%)

(n = 1,943).

Counterintuitively, Christians (65%) most "liked" the Gandhi quote, followed by those from another religion (57%) and then those with no religion (44%). Indeed, a larger proportion of Christians liked the Gandhi quote than the Bible verse (56%) (see Figure 3.4). One possible factor in this decision concerns how the wider members of one's social media network (e.g. Facebook friends) may respond to the image. If Gandhi (and the related quote) has greater acceptance, then it is the image that is less likely to cause any offence or impact the reputation of the individual who posts it.

With reference to the Bible verse that was shared, and taking the liked/disliked question as representative of the way in which the various religious groups responded, a familiar pattern emerges. Once again, the non-religious are most indifferent towards the Bible verse image (49% neither liked nor disliked), and nearly one in three (29%) disliked it. Those with a sense of religious identity liked it more (48% other religions, 56% Christians), although at least a third neither liked nor disliked it (34% other religions and 36% Christian). A minority also disliked the image, 29% of non-religious people did so, as too did 18% of those from another religion and 8% of Christians (see Figure 3.4).

The digital millennials who liked the image of the laughing man most were those of another religion (34% like, 34% dislike), followed by Christians (27% like, 36% dislike) and then the non-religious (17% like, 43% dislike). Thus it should not be assumed that a non-religious person is likely to appreciate something mocking the Bible. The non-religious were most likely to dislike all three images. One reason for this is that they may have considered all the images to be religious in nature so rejected them.

Finally, while churchgoers were the young adults most likely to affirm that the Bible is a supreme authority in their life, it should not be assumed that they reject anything that challenges the Bible, such as a mocking meme.

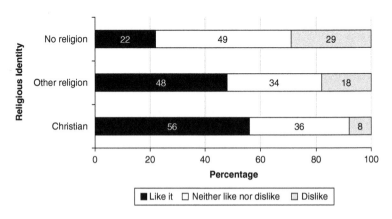

Figure 3.4 (Dis)like of the Bible verse in relation to religious identity (n = 1,879).

Most churchgoers (71%) liked the Gandhi quote, and over a quarter (27%) liked the laughing man image. It may be that some of these churchgoers did not feel threatened by these images and appreciated either the positive message that was communicated or were able to enjoy the humour.

Response to three online images

The second part of the question also referred to the three images and asked:

How likely or unlikely would you be to do the following in each case?

The participants were provided with five normal online responses and asked to indicate on a four-point Likert scale, from very likely to very unlikely, how they would respond. In this instance, contrasting with the previous question there was no midpoint option. There was a "don't know" response but fewer than 8% choose this possibly because they were being asked to indicate how they would practically respond to each image rather than how they felt about each (see Table 3.7).

Table 3.7 Practical response to the three images

Action	Likely	Unlikely	Don't know
Image 3—Gandhi Quote			
Ignore it	43%	50%	7%
Like it but not share it	39%	55%	7%
Share it	24%	70%	6%
Start a conversation with the person who shared it about the picture	18%	74%	8%
Block the person who shared it	12%	81%	6%
Image 1—Bible Verse			
Ignore it	50%	42%	7%
Like it but not share it	30%	63%	7%
Share it	21%	73%	7%
Start a conversation with the person who shared it about the picture	18%	74%	8%
Block the person who shared it	15%	79%	6%
Image 2—Laughing Man			
Ignore it	58%	35%	7%
Like it but not share it	20%	72%	7%
Share it	14%	78%	7%
Start a conversation with the person who shared it about the picture	14%	79%	7%
Block the person who shared it	18%	73%	9%

(*n* = 1,943).

Echoing the findings in the first part of this question, the Gandhi quote was most positively received, with 39% indicating they would "like it but not share it" and 24% who would share it. Then followed the Bible verse, with 30% liking but not sharing it and 21% sharing it, and finally the laughing man image, with 20% liking but not sharing it and 14% sharing it.

What can also be seen across all three images is a general disinterest because a common response was to ignore the images. Correspondingly, all three images were unlikely to be shared, an action usually indicating that what is being viewed is interesting or noteworthy. Indeed, they were unlikely to be "liked but not shared", an act that suggests something is valued but has less weight than sharing. It may be that digital millennials are not that interested in sharing these sorts of memes. It certainly fits with the data considered earlier indicating a general neutrality towards the six main religions in Britain today. It may therefore rehighlight the need to appreciate the indifference with which the Bible is held as being part of a wider indifference towards religion.

Concentrating on two responses ("ignore it" and "share it") as representative of the broader responses and focusing on the Bible verse data subdivided by religious identity, a familiar picture emerges. Non-religious young adults are most likely to ignore the Bible verse image (64%) and unlikely to share it (87%). Those from other religions and Christians are less likely to ignore it (36% other religion and 39% Christian) but are unlikely to share it (60% other religion and Christian) (see Figures 3.5 and 3.6).

Although non-religious digital millennials were most likely to ignore (64%) and not share the Bible verse (87%), they were also unlikely to block the person sharing it (83%). This supports the claim that many are treating this image with indifference. The existence of those who are unlikely to ignore the Bible verse (30% non-religious, 53% other religions and 55%

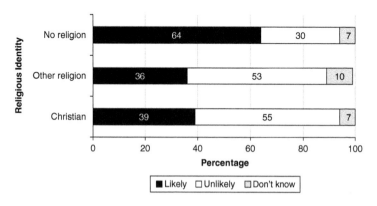

Figure 3.5 Likelihood of ignoring the Bible verse in relation to religious identity (*n* = 1,879).

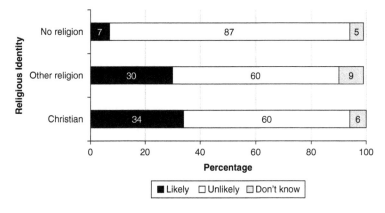

Figure 3.6 Likelihood of sharing the Bible verse in relation to religious identity (*n* = 1,879).

Christian) and are likely to share it (7% non-religious, 30% other religions and 34% Christian) reflects the positive qualification that has been highlighted. There were also some who would block the person sharing the Bible verse and this perhaps reflects the negative qualification. In this instance, it was those from other religions who were most likely to do this (11% non-religious, 23% other religions and 16% Christian).

Summary

A familiar pattern is emerging, with nearly half (48%) of all digital millennials either never or infrequently seeing a Bible verse on social media but 20% seeing them weekly (typically on Facebook). A third (32%) of digital millennials react positively to seeing a Bible verse on social media, 13% respond negatively, and 28% ignore it. Of those who have seen a Bible verse shared on social media, around half (51%) find it irrelevant, but 41% think it is a positive thing to do. When given three images to consider, there was a degree of indifference towards all three, but the Gandhi quote was preferred to the Bible verse, and the laughing man image was liked least.

Qualified indifference

The data presented in this chapter fits the picture earlier chapters have highlighted, for:

- 48% never or very infrequently see Bible verses being shared on social media.

- 51% of those who do see Bible verses on social media find them irrelevant and 46% do not pay attention to them.
- 42% responded neutrally, neither liking nor disliking the Bible verse image provided, and 50% said they would ignore it.
- 73% were unlikely to share, and 63% were unlikely to like but not share the Bible verse image.

These figures are compatible with an indifference towards religion in general and the Bible specifically. In this instance, it is manifesting itself as indifference towards Bible verses being shared on social media. This indifference was mainly, but by no means exclusively, seen among non-religious young adults.

Of course, there were those who engaged more positively with Bible verses on social media:

- 20% saw Bible verses weekly on social media.
- 32% react positively when they see such verses.
- 41% think that it is a positive thing to share Bible verses in this way.
- 38% liked the Bible verse image.
- 21% would have shared it.

This sizeable minority demonstrate the positive qualification that has also been highlighted in digital millennials' stance and engagement with the Bible. Christians and those of other religions were most likely to make up this group, with churchgoers being the most positive.

Finally, there were those who engaged more negatively with Bible verses on social media, demonstrating the negative qualification that is also required:

- 13% said Bible verses on social media irritated them or made them uncomfortable.
- 24% indicated it was a negative thing to share Bible verses on social media.
- 20% disliked the Bible verse image.
- 16% found it uncomfortable.
- 15% would block the person who shared it.

Once again it was the non-religious who were most likely to make up this group, but those belonging to a religion other than Christianity and indeed a number of Christians would also be included.

Secondary themes

The positive stance towards the Bible and relatively high level of Bible engagement noted among digital millennials from religions other than

Christianity continues to be seen in the viewing of Bible verses on social media. Those from other religions were not unequivocally positive about online Bible verses: 25% had never seen one; 16% react negatively when they do; and 24% think it is a negative thing to share Bible verses on social media. However, they (30%) and Christians (31%) were three times more likely to see Bible verses on social media compared to non-religious young adults (10%). Those from other religions were also three times more like to respond positively (39%) to seeing a Bible verse shared online than those with no religion (12%) and were three times more likely to describe them as relevant (28%) compared with non-religious young adults (8%). When given an example of a Bible verse image that might be shared on social media, they were twice as likely to like it (48%) compared with non-religious people (22%).

There also continued to be a lack of evidence that women were more religious than men, for example:

- 17% of women see Bible verses weekly on social media as do 24% of men. Correspondingly 52% of women never or don't know when they last saw a Bible verse on social media compared with 43% of men.
- 30% of women ignore a Bible verse when they see it on social media as do 27% of men.
- 29% of women respond positively to seeing a Bible verse on social media as do 34% of men.
- 39% of women and 38% of men liked the Bible verse image.
- 50% of women and 51% of men would ignore it and 18% of women and 23% of men would share it.

There were some brief instances where it could be argued that women were more Bible orientated than men, for instance 44% of women agreed that it is a positive thing for people to share Bible verses on social media compared with 38% of men, but this was rare.

It is noticeable that even though these were digital millennials who used social media weekly or more often, the data for viewing of Bible verses on social media mirrors the data for Bible engagement noted in Chapter 2. While the available responses were slightly different for each question, the general distribution of each data set is comparable (see Figure 3.7). This points towards a consistency between the young adults' social media Bible engagement and their other Bible engagement, for example, reading from a paper Bible or searching for a Bible passage on their smartphone. They were not more likely to encounter Bible verses in the digital world of social media.

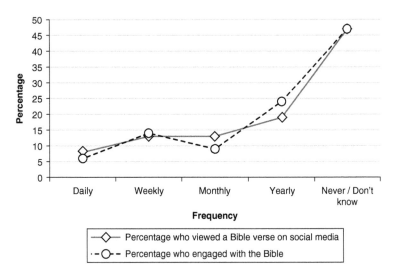

Figure 3.7 Comparison of Bible engagement and viewing Bible verses on social media.

Finally, while it may be assumed that most non-religious people would find a mocking meme of the Bible appealing because the Bible has been used in a derogatory way as a source for comedy (Meredith, 2015), this was not the case. Non-religious people were more likely to respond negatively to all three images, especially the laughing man one. There are many possible reasons for this. While the image is one that falls into an established genre of memes mocking or undermining an authority source (Bellar *et al.*, 2013), the lack of engagement may suggest they do not view the Bible as a current authority source they wish to challenge. It may also be that the meme communicates a message that is perceived as intolerant and attacks Christians. This may not sit well in a culture that values tolerance and a "live and let live" approach to human interaction. There may be a latent support for the Bible, or a sense that this cultural and social artefact needs to be treated with greater respect than that shown in the laughing man image. Yvonne Sherwood (2012) noted something similar with a Bible that was made available for annotation in an art exhibition at the Gallery of Modern Art (GOMA) in Glasgow. In that instance, some of the annotations were deemed to be offensive and following a public outcry, the Bible was removed and placed in a Perspex box. All of this points towards the need for further research into the place of the Bible in various aspects of British society and culture.

Conclusion

This chapter provides data from a third area of interaction between digital millennials and the Bible, and a consistent picture has emerged. The findings from this chapter reinforce the idea that indifference is one of the main responses these young adults have towards the Bible; half of them are unlikely to see a Bible verse shared on social media, and those who do typically find it irrelevant. However, both a positive and a negative qualification are required. Positively, there is a group, made up largely by the churchgoing cohort, who see Bible verses weekly on social media, and some of them would share the example Bible verse provided. Negatively, there is a smaller group, containing mainly non-religious people, who find that the sharing of Bible verses on social media makes them uncomfortable and irritates them.

This chapter also highlighted the existence of a social media filter bubble where religious people, in particular churchgoing Christians, were more likely to see Bible verses on social media than other groups. On account of some Christians being more Bible orientated than others, a second survey was designed to explore in more depth the Bible engagement of digital millennials who are very Bible orientated, and they are the subject of the next chapter.

4 Bible-centric digital millennials

Up until now, data from a nationally representative survey has been used to explore digital millennials' interactions with the Bible. Throughout the past three chapters, churchgoing Christians have been identified as those most positively disposed towards and engaged with the Bible (both online and offline). However, churchgoers are not a homogenous group; they span denominations and practices. This chapter considers those churchgoing Christians who are particularly Bible orientated. Following Field (2014), they are called "Bible-centric" Christians. The Bible plays a very significant role in the lives of these young adults and, by exploring their interaction with the Bible, insight is gained into the connection between those who are some of the greatest advocates for the Bible and the text itself. It also sheds light on the claim that digital millennials have a qualified indifference towards the Bible. In fact, at first glance, it brings it into question.

This chapter and the next move away from the style adopted in Chapters 1–3 whereby survey data was presented and then discussed mainly with reference to other Bible research. Chapters 4 and 5 continue to explore digital millennials and the Bible, but data from a Bible-centric group (Chapter 4) and the USA (Chapter 5) are brought into conversation with the data and findings presented in Chapters 1–3. By expanding our study into these areas, we draw upon wider research into the place of religion in British and American societies so as to more fully understand the phenomenon of qualified indifference.

The Bible-centric group

To consider this specific Christian cohort, the existing survey was adapted. Eight extra questions that explored in more detail the place of the Bible in the lives of the participants were added. This new online survey was disseminated at the same time as the nationally representative one. The social media networks of various Christian organisations were used to publicise the survey including: denominations (Methodist and Roman Catholic Church); parachurch organisations (Universities and Colleges Christian Fellowship, Student Christian Movement, Bible Society and the Evangelical Alliance); prominent Christians (Miriam Swaffield, Mark Russell and Rachel Jordan) and CODEC's own network. Nine hundred and sixty-eight individuals completed the survey, of whom 873 were churchgoing Christian digital millennials. This new data set has a margin of error of 3.3% at the 95% confidence interval.

As a group:

- 64% were female and 36% male.
- 39% were aged between 18 and 21, 35% were 22 to 27, and 26% were 28 to 35.
- Just under half described themselves as a "full-time student" (49%) and a third as working full time (35%).
- The top ethnic profiles were white—all (93%), mixed—all (3%), Asian—all (1%) and black—all (1%).
- 32% were Anglican, 16% Independent, 11% Baptists, 9% New Church, 7% Roman Catholic, 6% Methodist, 4% Pentecostal and 14% all others.
- 71% described themselves as "evangelical," 14% did not, and 16% were unsure.
- 43% lived in London or Southern England, 27% in middle England, 19% in Northern England and 11% in Northern Ireland, Scotland or Wales.
- 93% attended church at least weekly.

This group is not a representative sample of British Christian churchgoing digital millennials. The way the survey was disseminated drew on particular traditions and groups, as did its online nature. Thus, the data gathered had a higher proportion of white, female, students living in the South of England than the earlier churchgoing sample, who had the following composition:

- 43% were female and 57% male.
- 18% were aged between 18 and 21, 36% were 22 to 27, and 48% were 28 to 35.
- 15% described themselves as a "full-time student", and most said they were working (75%).
- The top ethnic profiles were white—all (79%), mixed—all (5%), Asian—all (5%) and black—all (11%).

- 16% were Anglican, 11% Independent, 8% Baptist, 3% New Church, 29% Roman Catholic, 4% Methodist, 10% Pentecostal, 18% all others.
- 18% lived in London or Southern England, 14% in middle England, 28% in Northern England and 13% in Northern Ireland, Scotland or Wales.
- 72% attended church at least weekly.

Those who completed the new online survey were a self-selecting group and because they all identified as Christian and attended church regularly, they could be thought of as a very specific subgroup located within the wider churchgoing cohort of the main survey. As will be demonstrated, they were highly engaged with the Bible and should be thought of as a "Bible-centric" research sample. Field (2014) uses this term to describe the degree to which the Bible plays a central role within in a particular group in society. In our case, it is being used as a descriptive label for a group who are very Bible orientated. This group has strong parallels with the "active affirmers" identified by Matthew Guest *et al.* in their study of Christianity and the British University experience. They define active affirmers as frequent churchgoers who have a committed personal faith, 70% of whom self-identify as evangelical or Pentecostal (2013, p. 41). The data produced by Bible-centric digital millennial Christians gives insight into a group who are passionate about the Bible, but we are not claiming they are representative of British Christianity.

The place of the Bible in their lives

To catch a glimpse of what role the Bible had played in their lives, these Christian young adults were asked two new questions that explored this indirectly. First:

Which, if any, of the following factors contributed positively and significantly to your decision to become a Christian? (Choose as many as required).

A list of 18 options was then provided, one of which was "reading or listening to the Bible" (see Table 4.1). The second question asked:

Which, if any, of the following activities, events, resources or experiences have been most helpful in your Christian life? (Choose as many as required).

Table 4.1 Influencing factors in becoming a Christian

Influencing factors	Percentage
Growing up in a Christian family	76%
Attending a church service	69%
Reading or listening to the Bible	63%
Conversation(s) with Christian(s)	59%
An experience of the love of Jesus	55%
Seeing God at work	53%
Attending a para-church group for youth or students (e.g. SU, CU, CathSoc)	42%
A particular life event or experience, whether positive or negative	40%
Being part of a church small group	37%
Participating in a mission or outreach team or other Christian project	26%
Dreams, visions or a spiritual experience	19%
Christian media (TV, radio, music, websites)	16%
A church's outreach program (e.g. youth cafe)	12%
Visiting/praying in a church open to the public (i.e. not during a service)	11%
Attending informal forms of church such as messy church or café church	11%
Going to an introduction to Christianity course like Alpha or Christianity Explored	9%
Other	9%
None of the above	0%

(*n* = 873).

One of the 21 different options provided was "personal Bible reading" (see Table 4.2). Both of these questions were built upon earlier ones that had been used among British Christians (Momentum, 2009, pp. 19–22; Evangelical Alliance, 2016, p. 23) and would provide two lenses through which the significance of the Bible could be evaluated in comparison to other activities. In both cases, people were asked to indicate as many factors or activities as necessary, and they were not limited to choosing their top three as was the case with some of the questions presented in the earlier chapters.

When asked about what factors influenced them to become a Christian, 63% identified reading or listening to the Bible. This was higher than being part of a small group (37%) or engaging with Christian media (including websites) (16%) but was lower than growing up in a Christian family (76%) (see Table 4.1).

Thus, for a majority of these young adults, the Bible played a significant role in their decision to become a Christian. What is noticeable is that the evangelistic activities undertaken by churches, such as an Alpha course (9%), messy church (11%) or an outreach program (12%) were less influential than

Table 4.2 Helpful activities in a Christian's life

Item	Percentage
Being part of a church	94%
Having Christian friends	85%
Praise and worship	78%
Sermons/teaching	77%
Personal prayer	71%
Personal Bible reading	71%
Seeing God at work	69%
An experience of the love of Jesus	61%
Being part of a church small group	67%
Reading Christian books (other than the Bible)	63%
Having other Christians in my family	57%
Listening to recorded Christian music	56%
Hearing others' testimony	49%
Having a Christian mentor, "soul friend" or accountability partner	46%
Participating in a mission or outreach team or other Christian project	45%
Being part of a parachurch group (e.g. SU, CU, CathSoc)	41%
Training sessions or courses to equip me for discipleship, mission or Christian service	37%
A particular life event or experience, whether positive or negative	33%
Dreams, visions or a spiritual experience	24%
Christian media (e.g. TV, radio, podcasts)	23%
Other	2%
None of the above	0%

(*n* = 873).

attending church (69%), reading or listening to the Bible (63%) or growing up in a Christian family (76%). This suggests that most of the cohort grew up within a Christian environment (e.g. with Christian parents who took them to church) rather than growing up in, say, a non-religious home and converting to Christianity. Other research has similarly highlighted the significance of the family in the transmission of Christian faith (Voas and Storm, 2012; Mark, 2016). In 2016 a British poll exploring what factors caused people to become Christians found that growing up in a Christian family (41%) was most significant, followed by attending church (28%), reading the Bible (27%) and talking with Christians (27%) (Evangelical Alliance, 2016, p. 23).[1]

When considering what activities these young adults find helpful in their Christian life, once again Bible engagement is significant, with 71%

1 The percentages are lower because those sampled could only identify up to three factors, whereas they were allowed to identify as many as appropriate in the Bible-centric digital millennial survey.

identifying reading or listening to the Bible as important to them. While this was not as high as being part of a church (94%), it was higher than experiencing the love of Jesus (61%), listening to Christian music (56%), training sessions for Christian service (37%) or Christian media (23%) (see Table 4.2).

Thus, the Bible played and plays a significant role in the lives of these young adults. What is also worth noting is that none of the popular items identified as important are specifically digital. This is intriguing, for it is the traditional aspects of Christian life that are identified as most influential or helpful—the impact of family, attendance at church and personal devotion (see also Foster, 2016). There may, of course, be digital dimensions to all of these; families stay in contact via social media, churches make use of multimedia technology, devotional material is accessed through a smartphone and so on. Nonetheless, digital innovations such as websites, blog posts and other aspects of modern Christian media, including TV and radio, were not especially significant (16%–23%).

When considering their stance towards and engagement with the Bible, the Bible-centric nature and practice of these young adults was further seen, especially when comparing them with the groups presented in the earlier chapters. Even the churchgoing group of Chapters 1–3 were less Bible orientated than the Bible-centric group, who were not only more Bible focused but attended church (93% weekly) more often than the churchgoing group did (72% weekly) (see Table 4.3).

The Bible-centric nature of this research sample stands in contrast to the normal picture that is painted of Christians' Bible engagement in Britain

Table 4.3 Comparison of Bible-centric young adults (Chapter 4) with churchgoing sample (Chapters 1–3)

Topic	Bible-centric group	Churchgoing group
Feel positive about the Bible	98%	75%
Agree the Bible should have supreme authority in guiding their beliefs, views and behaviour	78%	61%
Engage with the Bible at least weekly	95%	69%
What was the main reason for engaging with the Bible?	It brings me closer to God (32%)	To inspire me (15%)
See Bible verses shared on social media at least weekly	85%	53%
Think it is a positive for people to share Bible verses on social media	84%	69%

(Bible-centric group *n* = 873; Churchgoing group *n* = 319).

today. Recent surveys have produced headlines in national news outlets pointing to a lack of engagement and belief in the Bible:

- "Most Church of England Christians never read the Bible, survey finds" (Rudgard, 2017)
- "Resurrection did not happen, say quarter of Christians" (BBC, 2017)

The data from the self-selecting sample demonstrates that within British Christianity there are those who are very Bible orientated. We are not claiming that this is a large group or that they are increasing or decreasing in number but simply that they exist and are often ignored, played down or swamped by the greater numbers of Christians for whom the Bible does not play such an active role. Similar levels of Bible engagement have been noted by others, such as Bible Society who in a 2016 survey of over 3,500 British Christians found that 92% read (or listened) to the Bible weekly or more often (2016, p. 3). The Evangelical Alliance found that 80% of 18 to 37 year-olds Christians read the Bible weekly or more often (2015, p. 9). Both of these surveys were also based on self-selecting samples and so cannot be thought of as representative. They do however show the existence of a Bible-centric group within British Christianity.

Evangelicals

There was a difference in the significance of the Bible for those who identified as evangelical and those who did not. For example:

- 69% of evangelicals and 48% of non-evangelicals indicated that the Bible played a significant role in their decision to become a Christian.
- 80% of evangelicals and 48% of non-evangelicals identified personal Bible reading as important for their Christian life.
- 90% of evangelicals and 47% of non-evangelicals agreed that the Bible should have supreme authority in guiding their beliefs, views and behaviour.

There was less of a difference when their actual Bible use was considered:

- 98% of evangelicals and 88% of non-evangelicals engaged with the Bible at least weekly.
- 89% of evangelicals and 77% of non-evangelicals saw Bible verses on social media at least weekly.

The higher levels of Bible-centrism noted in the evangelicals is found, to different degrees, throughout the survey. It reflects an emphasis on the

Bible which evangelicals are noted for (Bebbington, 1989, pp. 3, 12–14) and evangelical organisations such as Christian Unions promote (Guest *et al.*, 2013, p. 148). This is one of the reasons why scholars have explored evangelicals' engagement with the Bible in some depth (e.g. Malley, 2004; Bielo, 2009; Rogers, 2015; Perrin, 2016).

Digital orientation

Bible-centric Christians were less digitally orientated in their general reading habits than the earlier churchgoing group. When asked about the technology used for their normal (i.e. everyday) reading, 72% of the Bible-centric group indicated paper and 6% principally made use of a digital device. This compares with 52% of churchgoers who read on paper and 15% who use digital technology.

It was also noted earlier in this chapter that digital media, such as websites or blogs, did not play a large role in their decision to become a Christian or in their Christian life. This was also noted, although to a lesser degree, when they were asked two questions concerning what resources they use to help them with the Bible. The first question asked:

What, if anything, do you typically do when you read or hear something from the Bible that you don't understand?

This question built upon a similar one used in an American context (Barna, 2016, p. 110) that was adapted. It provided a list of 13 options from which the participants were invited to choose up to three, ranking them accordingly.

Only one of the top five responses chosen was explicitly digital: it involved looking at online commentaries (16%). This was twice as popular as looking at printed commentaries (7%) but was not as common as thinking about it (32%), which perhaps reflects the Protestant-leaning of the sample. Praying about it (13%) along with asking a Christian friend (12%) were common responses as well (see Table 4.4).[2]

A second question that built upon earlier research (Evangelical Alliance, 2014, p. 13) asked:

Outside of a church context, which items or approaches, if any, do you typically use to help you engage with the Bible?

Once again, people were invited to select up to three responses from a list of 12 and rank them accordingly. As before, one of the top five responses

---

2 For consistency, the focus continues to be on the data provided by the first response.

Table 4.4 Response to not understanding part of the Bible

Action	Ranked first	Ranked in the top three
Think about it a lot	32%	55%
Look at online commentaries or study guides	16%	45%
Pray about it	13%	35%
Ask a Christian friend	12%	52%
Look at printed (paper) commentaries or study guides	7%	27%
Go online and see what other people think about the passage	5%	20%
Ask a pastor or church leader	5%	27%
Ignore it for the time being	4%	10%
Often nothing, because I usually find I understand enough of it	4%	12%
Often nothing, because I don't have to understand everything, sometimes I just accept it as true	2%	10%
Often nothing, because I don't feel like I have to believe every part of the Bible	1%	5%
Other	1%	1%
None of the above, because I never read, listen to or otherwise engage with the Bible	0%	0%

(*n* = 873).

picked was digital: accessing a website, blog or podcast (11%). In this instance, the paper alternative (a paper Bible-study or devotional notes) was more popular (16%). Yet neither were as prevalent as just reading the Bible (40%), with prayer and trusting the Holy Spirit (11%) and speaking to another Christian (7%) also being popular (see Table 4.5).

Table 4.5 Aids to Bible engagement

Item/Approach	Ranked first	Ranked in the top three
Just read the Bible	40%	63%
A paper Bible study or devotional notes	16%	33%
Prayer and trust the Holy Spirit	11%	50%
A website, blog or podcast	11%	35%
Speak to another Christian about the Bible reading	7%	51%
An online commentary or book	4%	19%
A paper commentary or other book	3%	17%
Emails from an organisation addressing the Bible passage	2%	7%
None—only engage with Bible in church	2%	4%
DVDs or other video resource	0%	3%
Other	2%	5%
None of the above	0%	1%

(*n* = 873).

Therefore, although these were young adults who owned digital devices, used social media regularly and had completed an online survey disseminated through social media networks, digital Bible engagement aids were not preferred to traditional non-digital ones. It is interesting that this group's approach to the Bible is one focused on reading the text and thinking about it. This is done prayerfully, with the input of others and with reference to online and offline resources.

Digital technology did not dominate their Bible engagement, and this can be traced through the survey data: 71% of them preferred the image of the paper Bible compared with 18% who preferred the image of the digital one. When they were asked about the Bible format they use, 57% indicated that they principally read a paper copy of the Bible. This was over three times higher than the most popular digital format (reading, watching or listening via a smartphone (16%)). The Bible-centric group were also asked:

What is your preferred format for engaging with the Bible?

To this, 77% indicated reading a print Bible. The degree of consistency between their responses to this question and the earlier one concerning the main Bible format they use demonstrates that these Bible-centric digital millennials clearly prefer a paper Bible (see Table 4.6).

Table 4.6 Main Bible format used in the last year and preferred Bible format

Format	Main Bible format used	Preferred Bible format
Read a physical copy of the Bible	57%	77%
Listened to someone else in the room read the Bible out loud	16%	2%
Read, watched, or listened to the Bible via a smartphone app	16%	13%
Searched for a Bible verse or passage on a smartphone	3%	2%
Read, watched, or listened to the Bible on an eReader/tablet	3%	3%
Searched for a Bible verse or passage on a laptop or desktop computer	2%	2%
Read, watched or listened to the Bible on a laptop or desktop computer	1%	1%
Listened to it or watched the Bible being read on TV or DVD	1%	0%
Searched for a Bible verse or passage on an eReader/tablet	0%	0%
Other	0%	1%

(n = 873).

There is therefore a cohort of British churchgoing young adults who are "digital millennials", yet their Bible engagement is not as digitally orientated as some might expect. This is not a complete rejection of the digital, but rather is probably a hybrid approach where both technologies are being used, perhaps depending upon the task required or convenience. John Weaver (2017) draws on the work of Ziming Liu (2008) to argue that paper Bible reading lends itself to a more intensive reading experience, which is a "sustained, in-depth, concentrated reading" (2017, pp. 251–252). Digital Bible reading, on the other hand, lends itself to extensive reading, which he describes as "scanning, spotting, searching" (p. 251). This may, in part, start to explain the preference for paper Bibles over digital ones among this group. It may reflect an intensive, thoughtful, engagement with the Bible, the kind of engagement Liu proposes is best achieved through paper. Once again though, further research is required to more fully understand the technological choices being made by these Christians.

Sharing Bible verses

When it came to social media, these young adults were highly likely to see Bible verses shared online, 85% doing so at least weekly, which is more than the churchgoing group considered in earlier chapters 53% of whom did (see Table 4.7).[3] Facebook (88%) was still the platform they were most likely to see these verses on.

They also found the sharing of Bible verses to be a positive thing, although in a different way and perhaps to a different degree than the churchgoing group. While the Bible-centric group were more likely to be encouraged

Table 4.7 Frequency of viewing Bible verses on social media, Bible-centric and churchgoing groups

Frequency	Bible-centric group	Churchgoing group
Daily	41%	25%
Weekly	45%	28%
Monthly	9%	24%
Once every six months	2%	7%
Once a year or less often	1%	3%
Don't know	2%	3%
Never	1%	10%

(Bible-centric group n = 873; Churchgoing group n = 319).

3 The algorithms used by social media companies may have a part to play here, as they are more likely to drive Bible posts to Bible-engaged users.

Table 4.8 Reaction to seeing a Bible verse on social media, Bible-centric and churchgoing groups

Reaction to seeing a Bible verse on social media	Bible-centric group	Churchgoing group
I feel encouraged	53%	29%
I ignore it	11%	7%
I feel comforted	6%	26%
I feel inspired	5%	24%
I feel irritated	5%	5%
I feel uncomfortable	3%	3%
Other	15%	2%
I have never seen a Bible verse shared on social media	0%	5%

(Bible–centric group *n* = 873; Churchgoing group *n* = 319).

when they saw a Bible verse on social media, the churchgoing group also found a significant degree of comfort and inspiration from online Bible verses (see Table 4.8).

However, this online Bible engagement is something these Bible-centric young adults were passive participants in rather than active instigators of, because they were asked:

Over the past year, how many times have you shared a Bible verse on social media, if at all?

Followed by:

Excluding church services and meetings, how many times have you shared a Bible verse in an offline (real-life) setting, if at all?[4]

Their responses to the first question indicate that only 7% shared a Bible verse on social media weekly or more often (see Table 4.9). This figure contrasts with the 85% who see Bible verses on social media at least weekly (see Table 4.7). In other words, these Christians are very likely to see Bible verses on social media but are unlikely to share them.

They were more likely to share a Bible verse in an offline setting, with around a third (36%) doing so weekly or more often (see Table 4.9). Since this excludes sharing during church services or meetings, it may indicate that some of these Bible-centric young adults are regularly discussing the Bible or a

4 Strictly speaking, online activity is no less "real life" than offline activity. There is though a popular tendency to equate offline with real life, and due to the public nature of the research, both terms were used in the survey question.

Table 4.9 Online and offline sharing of Bible verses

Frequency	Online sharing of Bible verse	Offline sharing of Bible verse
Daily	1%	2%
A few times a week	2%	18%
About once a week	3%	16%
About once a fortnight	4%	13%
About once a month	11%	18%
A few times a year	27%	22%
About once a year	19%	5%
Never	33%	5%

(*n* = 873).

biblical trope as part of their everyday conversations or in small-group settings. In other words, they are not averse to sharing Bible verses in certain contexts.

The difference between their online and offline sharing is consistent with the lack of digital Bible engagement that has already been noted with this group and further highlights the difference between their online and offline activity. They are sharing a lot more Bible verses in an offline (real life) setting, that is perhaps more private, than they are in an online (social media) setting, that may be more public. The low level of Bible verse sharing in an online setting is also seen in how the group reacted to the three images they were provided because they consistently responded less positively to all three images than the churchgoing group (see Figure 4.1). With reference to the Bible verse image, the Bible-centric group were three times more likely to dislike it and a third less likely to like it. This approximate distribution can be seen with regards to the laughing man image and the Gandhi quote as well.

In terms of how these young adults would practically respond to seeing the Bible verse image, 53% of the Bible-centric group indicated they would like but not share it, which is comparable with the 50% of churchgoers. However, the Bible-centric group were significantly less likely to share it (7%) compared with the churchgoing group (52%). This was not unique to the Bible verse image. The Bible-centric group were very unlikely to share the laughing man image (2%) and the Gandhi quote (6%) as well.

Therefore, although the Bible-centric group were more Bible orientated both in stance and in practice, when it came to sharing Bible verses on social media they shied away from this practice. Indeed, when they are compared with the groups explored in Chapters 1–3, the starkness of this is noteworthy. The following is the order of how likely the groups were to share the Bible verse image:

• 52% churchgoers
• 30% other religions

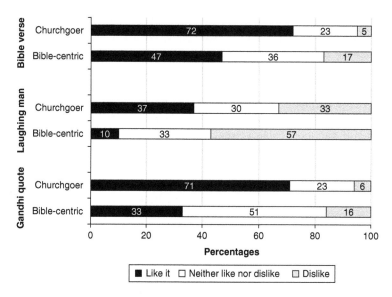

Figure 4.1 Bible-centric and churchgoers (dis)like of three images (Bible-centric group *n* = 873; churchgoing group *n* = 319).

- 18% non-churchgoers
- 7% non-religious
- 7% Bible-centric group

Even though they favour paper Bibles, it may be expected that the Bible-centric group would be the most likely to share Bible verses online, for they were positively disposed to the Bible and made substantial use of it. Moreover, as a group, they include a large number of evangelicals (71%), who believe it is important to share their faith with others. They are known for "conversionism" a belief that "lives need to change" (Bebbington, 1989, pp. 4–10), which results in evangelism. For instance, a recent survey of 1,703 active churchgoing millennials undertaken by the Evangelical Alliance[5] found that 77% "talked about their [Christian] faith with someone who wouldn't call themselves a Christian" (2015, p. 10). To that end, it may be supposed that the sharing of Bible verses coheres with this evangelistic emphasis. Hutchings captures this sentiment when noting that,

5 It is assumed that this self-selecting sample was predominantly made up of evangelicals.

from an evangelical perspective, "sharing even short passages of Biblical text can be a powerful spiritual act, exposing other people to the opportunity to hear and be changed by the Word while celebrating and attesting its value for the sharer" (2015b, p. 64). However, although the Bible-centric group are regularly viewing Bible verses online, they are not regularly sharing them. There are a number of potential reasons for this phenomenon. It may be that Bible-centric Christians feel that their status will be negatively impacted if they post Bible verses online or that the texts will stimulate a hostile response from their peers. If correct, this could challenge the hypothesis that digital millennials have a qualified indifference towards the Bible. This is because it points towards the possibility that the lived experience of Bible-centric Christians is that posting Bible verses online typically results in antagonism or ill favour rather than indifference. However, there are other possible reasons for this phenomenon which accord with our central claim. It may be that Bible-centric Christians' perceptions of how their peers will respond are overly negative. It is also possible that the actions (or online presence) of a small negative minority are sufficient to limit the Bible sharing of these Christians. Finally, it may also be the case that they are aware of the indifference that many of their peers have towards the Bible, so do not view the posting of Bible verses as a worthwhile endeavour. These reasons are briefly considered in the following pages.

Bible-centric Christians may be aware that most of their non-religious peers do not share Bible verses regularly online, so not to be seen as different, they modify their online behaviour. There is a common assumption that matters of faith and religion are principally private, and while Bible-centric Christians may not view faith in this way, they may assume that their peers do and would resonate with Steve Bruce and David Voas' claim that:

> the notion that religion should be a private matter for the individual and the family, very largely confined to the home and to the world of leisure, has become ever more firmly entrenched and only religion of the vaguest and most inoffensive kind is permitted in the public sphere.
>
> (2007, p. 6)

The public online sharing of Bible verses would be seen to break this code of keeping religion private and a similar code that condemns the imposing of religious views on other people. The posting of Bible verses on social media therefore deviates from the norm (Davie, 2002, pp. 45–47) and deviant behaviour is viewed at best as different and at worst as suspect and dangerous. It may therefore be the case that the individual who shares Bible verses on social media is in danger of losing social status and being maligned to some degree.

However, it could also be that these young adults are trying to avoid confrontation in what they understand to be a hostile environment. Bruce and Voas argue that what was once considered standard Christian teaching is now treated antagonistically by the mainstream British media. One example they give concerns a popular course on Christianity known as Alpha. There is nothing in the course that falls outside of established Christian creeds and practices. Yet "when pop star Geri Halliwell expressed an interest in Alpha, a Scottish Sunday paper used this headline for the story: 'Outrage over Geri's Links to Anti-Abortion, Anti-Gay Group'" (2007, p. 6). Kim Knott, Elizabeth Poole and Teemu Taira similarly note "the liberal press frequently represents Christianity as anti-egalitarian and out-of-date on issues of gender and homosexuality" (n.d, p. 1). Media portrayals of Christianity, along with the decline of church attendance, Bible belief, and so on, and changes to British society and legal system, such as the widespread acceptance of same-sex marriage, all may result in some Bible-centric Christians thinking of themselves as a religious minority in a post-Christian, hostile, secular country.

If Bible-centric Christians think that Bible verses shared online will be received negatively, this could challenge our central thesis that indifference is the normal response of digital millennials to the Bible. The data presented in the first three chapters suggests there is a small chance of an adverse reaction when sharing Bible verses on social media, (13% find it irritating or makes them uncomfortable) but more generally people are either indifferent (28% ignoring and 24% never seeing them) or are more positively disposed (32% find them comforting, inspiring or encouraging). If Bible-centric Christians' lived experience of sharing their faith in the past has resulted in negative feedback, then it is understandable if they no longer undertake such acts. All of which suggests that claims of qualified indifference may not accurately capture digital millennials' engagement and stance towards the Bible. It could be that those who completed the national survey gave more socially acceptable answers, ones that showed tolerance to religion in general, and the Bible in particular, rather than hostility. Similarly, they may have indicated how they would aspire to respond, rather than actually do. These are some of the weaknesses of large surveys based on self-reported beliefs and practices. If Bible-centric Christians perceive more antagonism towards the Bible than our data suggests, it may be that the data generated from the large national survey and the associated findings are inaccurate.

However, it could also be the case that Bible-centric Christians have mis-judged their peers and wider British culture. The existence of some who either indicated a willingness to share Bible verses online (as was the case with the churchgoing cohort of Chapters 1–3) or are sharing Bible verses on social media (Giles, 2016) demonstrates that negativity has not been, or is not imagined to be, the typical response. Bryony Taylor undertook an online survey of 300 Christians in 2013, in part to explore their online faith shar-ing, and she identified three groups of Christians (2016, p. 9). Those who:

1   "share their faith as something integrated into everything they do online"
2   "share faith online in an explicit way through sharing specifically Christian or overtly evangelistic content"
3   "share their faith largely through engagement with social justice issues and current affairs"

In her sample, a third directly shared overt Christian material and one assumes this would be lower if they typically received antagonistic responses. The belief that sharing Bible verses online would result in a negative response could therefore be misplaced, and the national survey data showing quali-fied indifference to the Bible may be correct.

It may also be that the small minority of digital millennials who respond negatively to online Bible verses is significant enough to limit the sharing of the Bible-centric group. In addition, other generations, such as Gen X, may be more sceptical towards the Bible, and their online responses may impact digital millennials' levels of sharing. This though does not cohere with the evidence of other Christians explicitly sharing their faith online, as noted above.

It is perhaps more likely that Bible-centric Christians are aware of a general indifference towards the Bible and so see little point in sharing something that is of little interest to their wider peers. Crossley recounts undertaking research into the reception of the Bible in Barrow-in-Furness, a town in northern England. He found participants were typically "baffled" and "bewildered" when they discovered his interest in the Bible (2016b, p. 33). It was noted earlier that 71% of the Bible-centric group identified as evangelical, and they are known for their emphasis on evangelism. While it could be assumed that sharing Bible verses online is a good evangelis-tic opportunity, this group potentially think of it as a poor evangelistic technique. If their peers are indifferent towards the Bible, then the sharing of Bible verses will spark little interest. Guest and his colleagues found something similar when exploring how Christian students belonging to the

Christian Union undertook evangelism. They noted that unlike the stereotypical street preaching call to turn or burn, what took place was "less confrontational, more irenic social outreach that fosters good relationships by not contravening the rules of social etiquette that prevail among the student population" (2013, p. 154).

Additionally, this group are selective in the medium through which they share their Bible verses, favouring face-to-face conversations (i.e. offline; 36% doing so weekly), rather than posting verses on social media (6% doing so weekly). Therefore, they may be adopting a more relational approach, making use of the relevant communication technology to suit their desired purpose. This accords with the digital aspect of their identity for a degree of technological sophistication is required to begin to differentiate the type and nature of technology that is best suited to the task required by the user. It also corresponds with what has been identified as one aspect of millennial identity, that they are highly relational (Rainer and Rainer, 2011).

The lack of sharing Bible verses online by the Bible-centric cohort therefore does not result in the rejection of qualified indifference as a finding, but it does show the need for further research (e.g. Phillips, *forthcoming*). Whatever the exact reasons why these Bible-centric Christians do not regularly share Bible verses online, a more in-depth exploration of their online identities and practices are required to clearly understand this phenomenon and the place of the Bible among this cohort of British society.

Conclusion

There is a group of digital millennials who are very Bible-centric. Other research indicates that this is not specific to the age profile of this cohort but rather points towards a subgroup within churchgoing Christianity. They are a group who can be overlooked in the conclusions drawn from national surveys. As a cohort, the Bible played and continues to play a dominant role in their lives. They were not as digitally orientated in terms of Bible engagement as their churchgoing peers from the main study. Indeed, while the digital did play a role in their lives, it was the more traditional aspects of Christianity that impacted them, such as attending church or having Christian friends. So too in terms of Bible engagement, they typically preferred to use paper Bibles than digital ones. This group did not share Bible verses on social media in a way that might be expected from a Bible-centric evangelical-heavy subgroup of society. This may be because to do so would negatively impact their social status or result in an antagonistic response. If so, it challenges the claim made in Chapters 1–3 that digital millennials are mainly indifferent towards the Bible. However, it may be the case that they have misjudged their peers or that they regard the sharing of Bible verses to be poor evangelism, and they are being selective in their use of technology. All of which would fall in line with qualified indifference. Ultimately, this phenomenon highlights the need for further research into the ways in which some Christians construct their social media presence and how they relate to the Bible.

5   A comparison with the USA

Thus far, the focus of any analysis has been on the British context. Chapters 1–3 explored the data of a nationally representative survey, and Chapter 4 concerned a group of Bible-centric Christians, all of whom lived in Britain. In this chapter, data from the USA is brought into conversation with the British data presented in the first three chapters. Comparing Bible engagement in one context (e.g. Britain) to another (e.g. the USA) can be helpful in highlighting differences and shining a spotlight on things that have previously gone unnoticed. In recent years, the American Bible Society has commissioned Barna[1] to undertake a yearly survey of Americans' Bible engagement, and these surveys provide data with which the British digital millennial findings can be compared. There are surveys based in other countries, for example Canada (Hiemstra, 2014), Australia (Huges and Pickering, 2010) and Norway (Rafoss, 2017). However, Barna's work along with a number of other American studies (Rainer and Rainer, 2011, pp. 238–240; Cole and Ovwigho, 2012; LifeWay Research, 2017; Goff, Farnsley II and Thuesen, 2017) provide a rich data source and therefore the best opportunity to make a meaningful comparison.

The Bible in the USA

In a recent anthology exploring the place of the Bible in the USA, Mark Noll summarises what he considers to be the central finding of a large national survey carried out in 2012. He writes:

> Almost half of the population report reading the Bible at least once at [sic] year, almost two-fifths at least monthly, over one-fourth at

---

1 Barna is "a research firm dedicated to providing actionable insights on faith and culture with a particular focus on the Christian church" (Barna, 2015, p. 175).

least weekly, and about 10 percent daily. So there are more readers of the Bible each and every day than the record-breaking number of Americans who watched the recent World Cup final.

(2017, p. 343)

There is good reason for his upbeat tone. First, these findings refer specifically to reading the Bible outside of a church service. In other words, the act of Bible reading is probably a direct and conscious one. Second, when asked the reason for engaging with the Bible, the main response was for personal prayer and devotional purposes. This is considered good news if, like Noll, you are a practising Christian and view Bible reading as a worthwhile activity.

While the data for millennials is lower than the national average, only 44% read the Bible yearly or more often, nonetheless the summary above lends itself to the narrative that a lot of Americans are reading the Bible and are doing so for religiously orientated reasons (Noll, 2017, p. 342). This runs against the more common claim of decline which can be seen in headlines such as:

- "Americans Are Fond of the Bible, Don't Actually Read it" (Smietana, 2017)
- "The Scandal of Biblical Illiteracy" (Mohler, 2016)
- "The Epidemic of Bible Illiteracy in Our Churches" (Stetzer, 2015)

The percentages provided by Noll correspond with Barna's recently published analysis of the Bible in America. This is a collation of six years' worth of Bible surveys and they found that outside of a church setting, for millennials (2016, pp. 101, 144):

- 9% read the Bible daily.
- 18% one to four or more times a week.
- 8% monthly.
- 19% one to four times a year.
- 45% less than once a year or never.

There is a similarity between these figures and the British context as presented in Chapter 2, for in Britain:

- 6% engage with the Bible daily.
- 14% once or a few times a week.
- 9% once or twice a month.

- 24% once or a few times a year.
- 47% never.

At least six significant qualifications are required, however. The Barna survey asked:

> *How often, if ever, do you actually read the Bible, not including times when you are at a church service or church event?*

Whereas the British survey asked:

> *Over the past year, how often have you read, listened to, or otherwise engaged with the Bible, if at all (including during church services and special occasions e.g. weddings and funerals)?*

Note first that the Barna survey specifically captures levels of Bible reading and does not extend to listening (or watching). The British survey, on the other hand, indicates that all forms of Bible engagement, be that reading, listening or watching, are to be included. Second, the America survey focuses on Bible reading outside of a church context. In other words, it is more likely to indicate levels of personal Bible reading. The British survey, however, made clear that all forms of Bible engagement were to be included: personal Bible reading is one form but listening to the Bible in a church service or at a special occasion would be equally noteworthy. Third, among the Barna surveys, 67%–78% of the sample identify as Christian (about one-third of these Christians are practising and two-thirds non-practising[2]) and 22%–33% are identified as non-Christian (Barna, American Bible Society, and InterVarsity Christian Fellowship, 2014, p. 77). These figures are reversed in the British survey where 35% identify as Christian (approximately half of whom are regular churchgoers, and half are not) and 62% as non-Christian. Thus, the British data accounts for a wider variety of Bible engagement, but proportionally the USA Bible reading results represent a larger cohort of the population.

Fourth, the age of a "millennial" often varies according to the survey. Barna focused on those aged 18 to 32, while the British survey was open to those aged 18 to 35. Fifth, it is also the case that the religious profile of each group is different. Barna excludes Mormons and Jehovah's Witnesses

---

2 Barna defines a practising Christian as one who says their faith is very important to them and attends church at least monthly.

from its "Christian" category, for although both groups self-identify as Christian, they are not viewed as such by mainstream Protestant and Catholic churches. The British survey included both these groups within its "Christian" category. Sixth, even how Americans and British people respond to religious surveys is said to be different (Davie, 2002, pp. 28–29). Notwithstanding these caveats, there is enough of an overlap for a meaningful, if provisional, comparison to take place. Indeed, the British digital millennials survey was developed in light of some of the questions used in American surveys.

This demonstrates that a degree of caution is required when comparing questions from different surveys of different people groups. There is benefit in comparing people's responses to specific questions in British and American Bible surveys, but a simple comparison may not always account for other factors that shape both the production and interpretation of the data. A way of undertaking a comparison that minimises these issues is to focus on the conclusions drawn by the different studies, for they should present the key findings in general terms, and these generalisations can then be compared. Therefore, what follows mainly compares the conclusion presented in Chapters 1–3 with those Barna has reached in the USA. This will provide a robust if initial comparison of young adults' Bible engagement in both countries.

The Bible in Britain: a summary

The argument made in Chapters 1–3 was that most digital millennials are indifferent towards the Bible:

- 40% felt neither positive nor negative about it.
- 58% had no question to ask about the Bible.
- 62% said they had little or no relationship with it.
- 61% engaged with the Bible once a year or less.
- 57% see Bible verses on social media yearly or less (or can't remember).
- 53% ignore or never see Bible verses on social media.
- 42% neither liked nor disliked the Bible verse image.
- 50% would ignore it.

A minority are positively orientated towards the Bible:

- 38% felt positive about the Bible.
- 21% agreed that it should be a supreme authority in their life.

- 13% described their relationship with the Bible as exciting or very close.
- 20% engaged with the Bible at least weekly.
- 20% see Bible verses on social media at least weekly.
- 32% feel inspired, encouraged or comforted when they see a Bible verse on social media.
- 38% liked the Bible verse image.
- 21% would share it.

A smaller minority are negatively orientated towards it:

- 16% felt negative about the Bible.
- 13% feel irritated or uncomfortable when they see a Bible verse on social media.
- 24% think it is a negative thing to share Bible verses on social media.
- 20% disliked the Bible verse image.
- 15% would block the person who shared it.

In light of these findings, the distribution of the data suggests that approximately 50%–60% of digital millennials are indifferent towards the Bible, 25%–35% are more positively disposed to it and 10%–20% are more negatively disposed (see Figure 5.1).

This distribution is tentative. The survey questions were not designed to test for indifference but were broad allowing for the exploration of the Bible and digital millennials from multiple angles. Therefore, this conclusion requires further examination and refinement. Nevertheless, in light of the data that was produced, an indicative profile can be outlined. It serves as a snapshot of digital millennials' stance towards and engagement with the Bible, and as a stimulus for further study.

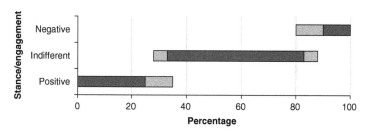

Figure 5.1 Qualified indifference (*n* = 1,943).

The Bible in America: a summary

Barna's six-year study of the Bible in America produced similar results to those Noll refers to (2017, p. 343). However, it was less positive in its summary due to the longitudinal decline of Bible engagement that they identify, something the survey quoted by Noll did not. Barna (2016, p. 152) summarises its research stating that, of all American millennials (see also Figure 5.2):

12% are Bible engaged	Typically view the Bible as the actual or inspired word of God, and engage with it at least four times a week.
36% are Bible friendly	Typically view the Bible as the actual or inspired word of God, and read it less than four times a week.
27% are Bible neutral	Typically view the Bible as the inspired word of God or the words of man, and rarely or never read the Bible.
25% are Bible sceptic	Typically view the Bible as just another book written by men and rarely or never read it.

While just under half are identified as "Bible Engaged" or "Bible Friendly", approximately a quarter are labelled "Bible Neutral" and another quarter "Bible Sceptic". The label "Bible Neutral" mainly concerns a lack of Bible engagement. Approximately 50%[3] of this group believe that the Bible has errors but is the inspired word of God, which suggests a positive disposition rather than neutrality. The term "Bible Sceptic" implies a degree of doubt or cynicism but this label is not being used to denote a negative disposition but rather that the Bible is rarely used and is viewed as a book like any other. As a group, however, 50% indicate that the Bible has too much influence on American society,[4] which may reflect a degree of negativity towards the Bible.

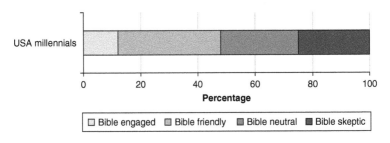

Figure 5.2 American millennials' Bible engagement profiles (data from 2010–2016).

---

3 Data for millennials is unavailable, so this percentage refers to the entire adult sample.
4 Data for millennials is unavailable, so this percentage refers to the entire adult sample.

More recently in 2017, Barna added a fifth element to its schema: "Bible Hostile", which refers to those who believe the Bible was written to manipulate or control people and so are negatively disposed towards the Bible. The figures for millennials in 2017 were approximately (American Bible Society, 2017, p. 41; see Figure 5.3):

- 14% Bible engaged
- 38% Bible friendly
- 24% Bible neutral
- 8% Bible sceptical
- 16% Bible hostile

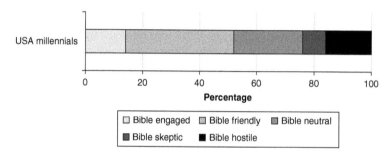

Figure 5.3 American millennials' Bible engagement profiles (data from 2017).

What the Barna surveys have thus far failed to identify is any indifference towards the Bible, but in 2018, a new algorithm was used to draw out more distinctions between different types of engagement.[5] It analysed responses to 14 questions and divided people into five different categories (American Bible Society, 2018, pp. 5–7, 32). With reference to millennials, the distribution is as follows (see Figure 5.4):

- 6% Bible centered
- 17% Bible engaged
- 17% Bible friendly
- 7% Bible neutral
- 53% Bible disengaged

Two new categories are introduced: "Bible Centred", which refers, in part, to adults who usually attend church weekly and typically read the Bible

5 Thanks to Brooke Hempell (Barna's SVP for Research) for clarifying this, via personal communication on 10 October 2018.

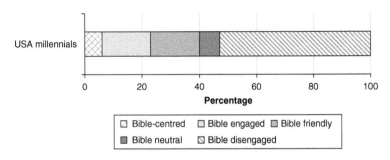

Figure 5.4 American millennials' Bible engagement profiles (data from 2018).

daily; and "Bible Disengaged", being those who infrequently engage with the Bible and indicate that it minimally impacts their lives. Barna points out that "those in the Bible Disengaged category do not necessarily have hostile or negative feelings toward the Bible but may simply be indifferent" (American Bible Society, 2018, p. 7). However, some in this category view the Bible positively: 43% (very) strongly agree that the Bible is a rulebook or guide on how to live their best life (2018, p. 40).[6]

This new analysis finds that just over half of millennials rarely use the Bible and say it has little or no impact on their lives. This was not unique to them; it was also the case for the population in general. While this representation of the data identifies a large degree of disengagement (and possible disinterest) with the Bible, which the earlier surveys had not drawn out, what is lost is the negative disposition that had earlier been identified as "Bible Hostile".

British and American comparison

What then can be concluded from these summaries? First, a large proportion of American millennials are positively disposed towards or engaged with the Bible, perhaps anywhere between 60% and 70%. This is based on all those identified as Bible Centred, Engaged, Friendly and 40% of those who are labelled Neutral—as many in this group view the Bible as the inspired word of God but with errors. Second, a minority are negatively disposed towards the Bible, perhaps between 10% and 20%. This is based on those who are identified as Bible Hostile and think that it was written to control and manipulate people. Third, therefore in light of this perhaps between 20%

6 Data for millennials is unavailable, so this percentage refers to the entire adult sample.

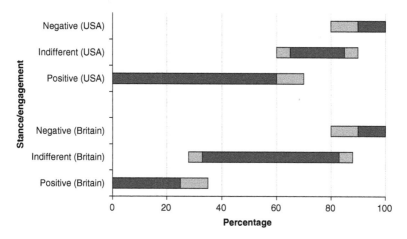

Figure 5.5 American and British millennials' Bible engagement profiles (summary).

and 30% of American young people are indifferent towards the Bible. This is based on the size of the positive and negative groups and on those identified as Bible Disengaged, Neutral and Sceptic—many of whom rarely engage with the Bible and view it as a book written by humans (see Figure 5.5).

While further research is required to more clearly determine the exact size of each group, nonetheless, in general terms, a larger percentage of American millennials are positively disposed to and/or engaged with the Bible compared with British millennials. A similar number of millennials from both countries are negatively disposed towards the Bible. Finally, a smaller percentage of American millennials are indifferent towards the Bible than their British peers. This summary is a tentative one, distilled from the conclusions that Barna has reached over the past three years. Nevertheless, it is based on the most recent research and provides an initial summary of Bible engagement in the USA and Britain among young adults. It also points toward the need for further bespoke comparative research into Bible engagement in these two countries.

Non-Christian millennials in the USA and Britain

The comparison between the USA and Britain needs to be understood in light of each country's religious context, as highlighted earlier in this chapter. Between 67% and 78% of millennials in the USA identify as Christian, twice as many as in Britain (35%). The large number of American Christians parallels the large degree of positivity towards the Bible that has been identified above (see Figure 5.5). So too in Britain the large group of non-religious digital millennials (48% of the population) accounts for the large degree of indifference. What is perhaps more surprising is that although the USA has proportionally half the number of millennials who identify as not religious or with a religion other than Christianity (22%–33%) compared with Britain (62%), nevertheless a similar level of negativity towards the Bible is noted in both countries. It is those who identify with no religion, and at times with one other than Christianity, who are most likely to view the Bible negatively. This can be seen in Barna's data tables (e.g. Barna, American Bible Society and InterVarsity Christian Fellowship, 2014, pp. 5, 8; American Bible Society, 2017, pp. 67–68) and in Chapters 1–3 of this book. It therefore could be suggested that proportionally in America there is a higher concentration of negative sentiment towards the Bible by non-Christians compared with Britain, for fewer of them are producing proportionally the same level of negativity.

Barna uses the label "non-Christian" to describe those who identify with no religion and a religion other than Christianity. The majority (82%) of Barna's non-Christian group is made up of people who are not religious and the remaining 18% identify with another religion (of which 38% identify as Mormon).[7] To provide as close a comparison as possible with the British data, the "no religion" and "other religion" groups from the British digital millennial survey were drawn together ($n = 1,198$) and that joint data used for comparative purposes. Around three-quarters of this sample (78%) identified as not religious and one quarter (22%) with another religion (the largest being Islam with 44%). Contrasting the Barna cohort, this group does not include Mormons and Jehovah's Witnesses, and for the sake of simplicity, the label "non-Christian" is also used.

What follows brings data sources from the USA and Britain together to explore non-Christians' response to some specific questions and more importantly the conclusions that have been drawn about them. In both countries, non-Christians are unlikely to engage with the Bible, around two-thirds reading/engaging either once a year or never but around one in eight doing so weekly or more often, (see Table 5.1).

Notwithstanding the differences mentioned earlier, there is a similarity in the profile of both data sets. The Bible is rarely engaged with frequently and is more likely to be engaged with yearly if at all.

However, when Barna brought together data from various questions and surveys, it concluded that non-Christian millennials in the USA "hold ambivalent or sometimes quite negative views of the Bible and of those

7 Thanks to Brooke Hempell for this information, via personal communication 6th June 2018.

Table 5.1 Non-Christian Bible engagement in the USA and in Britain

	USA millennial non-Christians	British millennial non-Christians
	How often do you use the Bible on your own, not including times when you are at a large church service or Mass?	Over the past year, how often have you read, listened to, or otherwise engaged with the Bible, if at all (including during church services and special occasions)?
Daily	6%	4%
A few times a week	3%	4%
Once a week	4%	4%
Once a fortnight	Not available	3%
Once a month	3%	3%
A few times a year	4%	7%
Once (or twice) a year	7%	13%
(Less than once a year) or Never	73%	62%

USA *n* = 294, based on 2018 State of the Bible in America research[8]; Britain *n* = 1,198.

who read it. For many non-Christian millennials, the Bible's "brand" is negative" (Barna, 2016, p. 122). For example, when asked to choose which statements came closest to describing their belief about the Bible, the top three responses by non-Christians were (Barna, American Bible Society and InterVarsity Christian Fellowship, 2014, p. 8):

1 The Bible is a useful book of moral teachings (30%).
2 The Bible is a dangerous book of religious dogma used for centuries to oppress people (27%).
3 The Bible is an outdated book with no relevance for today (19%).

Data on how people respond to seeing Bible verses shared on social media are similarly negative. When asked: What do you think when you see other people quote scripture in their social media or blogs? The top three responses by non-Christian millennials were (Barna, 2016, p. 121):

1 It bothers me if they use verses naively or out of context (35%).
2 I think it's okay sometimes if you are religious (33%).
3 I find it irritating (30%).

8 Thanks to Brooke Hempell for this information, via personal communication 10th October 2018.

With regard to seeing someone read the Bible in public, Barna comments that:

> the primary feelings non-Christians experience are alienation and distance. Non-Christian millennials say they assume the Bible reader is politically conservative (22%); that they don't have anything in common with the person (21%); that the person is old fashioned (17%); or that he or she is trying to make a statement or be provocative (15%).
>
> (2016, p. 120)

This negativity is in part captured by those Barna identified as "Bible Hostile" in the 2017 survey. Therefore, the conclusion reached in the USA is that non-Christians are quite negatively disposed towards the Bible, viewing it as a dangerous or outdated book, being bothered or irritated when they see Bible verses shared on social media and distancing themselves from someone who reads the Bible in public.[9]

This contrasts British non-Christian millennials, for in accord with the conclusion reached in Chapters 1–3 their main response is indifference. Some were negatively disposed to various aspects of the Bible, but a similar number were positively disposed to it, these two groups, though, were in the minority. Indifference was the main response:

- 55% felt neither positive nor negative towards the Bible (or did not know how they felt), 22% felt negative towards the Bible and 23% felt positive.
- 63% did not have a relationship with the Bible, 12% described it as minimal and 6% described it as exciting or very close.
- 62% had not read, listened to or otherwise engaged with the Bible over the past year, a further 20% had only done so once or a few times a year, but 11% did so weekly or more often.
- Of those who engaged the Bible at least once in the last year, 22% did so at a special church service and 18% don't know why they engaged with it. The third-highest reason given was for comfort (8%).
- 35% typically ignore a Bible verse on social media, 16% respond negatively and 18% respond positively.
- 41% didn't know if it was a positive or negative thing to share Bible verses on social media, 32% said it was a negative thing and 28% said it was a positive thing.
- 46% neither liked nor disliked the Bible verse image, 27% disliked it and 28% liked it.

9 See David Kinnaman's *UnChristian* (2007) for Barna research among millennials highlighting the extent to which non-Christians also hold negative view of Christians and Christianity in general.

Barna does note that non-Christian Americans are also indifferent towards the Bible. Indeed, there is also evidence that some in this group view the Bible positively: 27% identify it as inspired or pointing to God in some way; 30% believe it to be a useful book of moral teachings; and 17% wish they read the Bible more (Barna, American Bible Society and InterVarsity Christian Fellowship, 2014, pp. 8, 30). In part, this positive disposition reflects the inclusion of Jehovah's Witnesses and Mormons within the non-Christian cohort. The overarching claim, however, is that millennials in the USA hold "ambivalent and sometimes extremely negative views about the Bible" (Barna, 2014). This is not the case in Britain where non-Christian digital millennials predominantly hold ambivalent or indifferent views of the Bible. There is some negativity attached to it, but this is not the dominant finding. Indeed, the degree of negativity is similar to the degree of positivity. It would therefore appear that non-Christians in the USA are more antagonistic towards the Bible than their British peers. This corresponds with the observation earlier that there are proportionally half the number of non-Christians in the USA compared with Britain, but a similar level of negativity is noted in both countries (see Figure 5.5).

This comparison highlights the significance of indifference for British millennials, and non-Christians in particular. Further comparison with the USA sheds light on three reasons for the dominance of indifference in Britain and negativity in the USA among non-Christians. The first concerns the politicisation of religion that has occurred in the USA but has not in Britain, at least not to the same degree. Peter Berger *et al.* argue that in response to a liberal elite who were driving a more secular and liberalising agenda in the USA the "religious right" arose. These were conservative Christians (typically) who felt that their religious and moral values were being eroded by politicians and the judiciary, for example, the Supreme Court. The emergence of the religious right was marked by political activism and the elevation of religious voices clustered around certain social/moral issues, such as abortion. The result has been the polarisation of a country, with religious conservatives on one side typically aligning themselves with the Republican party and secular liberals on the other identifying with the Democratic party (2008, pp. 126–128). Others have noted this politicisation of religion in the USA and its polarising effect. Landon Schnabel and Sean Bock (2017) build on the work of Michael Hout and Claude Fischer (2014) to argue that since the 1980s the tying together of religion and politics has resulted in the decline of moderate forms of religiosity and the strengthening of more intense forms. While surveys do show that many in the USA hold moderate views on moral issues (Berger *et al.*, 2008, pp. 127–128), what is significant for our purposes is that the result of polarisation is the strengthening of intense opinions and (non)religious views and practices. In Britain, there has not been the same extent of politicisation of religion. Bruce and Voas argue that "in contrast to the polarisation found in the US, the public position of organised religion in the UK is not generally contentious" (2007, p. 3). There is not the same culture of invoking religious symbols, such as the Bible, to further a particular cause or agenda. It does happen (Crossley, 2016a; Edwards, 2015), but to a lesser degree. This starts to explain why non-Christians in the USA are more negative towards the Bible and those in Britain are more indifferent.

Second, religious identities, beliefs and actions are also more public facing in the US, in that they are part of the religious/political/social discourse. To that end, someone's religious identity is "a fundamental category of identity and association" there (Berger *et al.*, 2008, p. 30). This contrasts the British context which holds that religious identity, beliefs and actions are less significant and assumed to be principally a private rather than public matter. In Britain, there is an implicit rule that "you are completely free to live by your religion in private, but keep it out of the public sphere" (2008, p. 130). Therefore, while Bible-centric Christians in Britain are unlikely to share Bible verses on social media (Chapter 4), this is something many practising Christians undertake in the USA (see Table 5.2).[10]

Chapter 4 noted that approximately 6% of British Bible-centric Christians post Bible verses online at least weekly, but over four times as many practising Christian Americans do (26%). Religion, therefore, plays a less public role in the lives of British millennials, all of which lends itself to indifference. In the USA, however, it is more acceptable for religion to be public facing. Therefore, non-religious people draw on their sense of non-religious identity and associated values when engaging publicly. This in turn

Table 5.2 Frequency of sharing Bible verses in the USA and in Britain

Frequency of online sharing of Bible verses	American practising Christians	British Bible-centric Christians
Daily	13%	1%
A few times a week	13%	2%
About once a week	Not available	3%
About once a fortnight/a few times a month	25%	4%
About once a month	Not available	11%
A few times a year	30%	27%
About once a year	Not available	19%
Never	19%	33%

10 For a wider exploration of faith sharing on social media in the USA, see Barna, 2018.

encourages, and is encouraged by, a politicisation of religion and contributes to non-Christians' higher levels of negativity towards the Bible.

Third, the religious profile of both countries is another factor. In Britain non-religion is a majority position and is on the increase (Woodhead, 2016).[11] Christians are in the minority. Some non-religious people may feel that Christianity is too imbedded in British life (e.g. there is still a state church), so they view it as a threat or as overreaching itself; others though will not. It is perhaps more likely that most will view it as having little personal significance, in other words they are indifferent towards it. They probably do not disapprove of others engaging with it and may want the right to access parts of it themselves, say for a wedding, if they so desire. However, in the USA to identify as non-religious or with a religion other than Christianity is to be in the minority. Christians are in the majority. It may be reasoned that the minority groups are aware of their status, so some may feel the need to highlight their (non)religious distinctives. Others may in some way feel threatened by the dominant group and associated cultures with which they do not identify. Their response may not only involve the refusal to acquiesce to the norms promoted by Christians, such as viewing the Bible as authoritative but to critique and challenge those norms and values as well. David Kinnaman (Barna's president) writes: "[Y]ou have to keep the overwhelming size of American Christianity in mind because part of the reason that people [non-Christian Americans] agitate against the Christian faith is due to the real—and perceived—position of influence it has had" (2007, p. 17).

Therefore, in Britain religion has not been politicised to the same degree as it has in the USA, it is also a more private matter and non-religion is the majority religious identity. All of these factors facilitate an indifference towards religion by non-Christians in Britain. In the USA, however, the politicisation of religion along with its public nature and the minority status of non-Christians help explain the degree of negativity non-Christian Americans express towards the Bible.

Conclusion

The profile of American and British millennials' engagement with the Bible is different. Americans are more likely to view the Bible positively while the British are more likely to treat it indifferently, and this reflects the religious profiles of both societies. However, there is a small minority in both countries who view the Bible negatively. Those holding this view are more likely

---

11 Non-religion is growing in the USA as well (Voas and Chaves, 2016).

to be non-Christians, and in America, they make up a smaller percentage of the population than they do in Britain. However, a similar degree of negativity is being produced suggesting that, in general, non-Christians in America are more antagonistic towards the Bible than their British counterparts. This corresponds with the central thesis of indifference that Chapters 1–3 have demonstrated, for British non-Christians are most likely to be indifferent towards the Bible, whereas American non-Christians are more likely to view the Bible with a significant degree of negativity. The comparison sheds light on three reasons for the indifference noted in Britain: that religion is not as politicised in Britain; that it is viewed as being a private matter and that non-religious people are in the majority.

6 Conclusion

Digital millennials treat the Bible with qualified indifference. This was seen throughout Chapters 1–3, when compared with a Bible-centric group in Chapter 4 and contrasted with American Bible engagement in Chapter 5. Throughout those chapters, the need for further research has been consistently highlighted. The main themes that have been traced throughout the book are now brought together and explored in light of contemporary theories of religion. While this inevitably results in the raising of further research questions, it also highlights some of the implications of this study for religiosity in Britain today and the place of the Bible in British society.

Qualified indifference: summary

Chapters 1–3 demonstrated that a large proportion of digital millennials are indifferent to the Bible:

- feeling neither positive nor negative about it (40%)
- having little or no relationship with it (62%)
- rarely engaging with it (61%)
- ignoring or never seeing Bible verses on social media (53%)
- neither liking nor disliking the Bible verse image used in the survey (42%)

A smaller proportion are more positively disposed to the Bible:

- feeling positive about it (38%)
- describing their relationship with it as exciting or very close (13%)
- engaging with it weekly (20%)
- feeling inspired, encouraged or comforted when they see a Bible verse on social media (32%)
- liking the Bible verse image (38%)

A smaller proportion again are more negatively disposed to it:

- feeling negative towards it (16%)
- feeling irritated or uncomfortable when they see a Bible verse on social media (13%)
- disliking the Bible verse image (20%)
- thinking it is a negative thing to share Bible verses on social media (24%)

In light of this and other data presented earlier, it is suggested that 50%–60% of digital millennials are indifferent towards the Bible, 25%–35% are more positively disposed towards it and 10%–20% are more negatively disposed. Chapter 1 noted that comparable studies into the place of the Bible in British society also highlight qualified indifference, although they do not use this term. Reflecting on the Bible surveys which made up his meta-analysis Field notes that "the Bible has been viewed as increasingly less significant in personal lives and less relevant to the needs of modern society" (2014, p. 518). This indifference has been identified in smaller studies as well (Spencer, 2005; Crossley, 2016b). Surveys often also indicate a significant but "small and dwindling minority" (Field, 2014, p. 517) who view the Bible positively and an even smaller group who are more antagonistic towards it. Therefore, the conclusion reached from our study corresponds with the findings from other Bible research.

Qualified indifference: the need for further research

The earlier chapters briefly pointed towards the profile of those who make up qualified indifference. Those with no religion were most likely to be indifferent towards the Bible and they were also most likely to be negatively disposed towards it. The people who were most likely to engage positively with the Bible were churchgoing digital millennials, although some non-churchgoers and those of other religions also treat the Bible in this way. This profile resonates with other research that considers the Bible's value to the British public (Spencer, 2005; Bruce and Voas, 2007). Further research is required to understand more clearly the profile of these groups and the factors that result in some people being indifferent to the Bible and others feeling negatively or positively disposed towards it.

The data starts to do this for the non-religious group because it can be subdivided according to the extent to which they (dis)agreed with the following statement:

I have my own way of connecting with the Divine without churches or religious services.

This is a question used in the European Values Study and is one way of exploring how spiritual people are. Of the non-religious cohort, 31% disagreed with the statement and could be labelled "not religious and not spiritual" and 16% agreed with it and so could be thought of as being "spiritual but not religious". Finally, the remaining either indicated "not applicable" (36%), "don't know" (8%) or neither affirmed nor rejected the statement (8%).[1] Throughout the study, those young adults who were not religious and not spiritual responded more negatively to the Bible than those who identified as spiritual but not religious (see Table 6.1).

This demonstrates that some non-religious people are more likely to respond negatively towards the Bible than others, and further research is required to delineate how people are responding and the reasons for this.

Further study is also required to more clearly grasp whether these young adults were more or less indifferent, or positive or negative towards the Bible than other generations. The established narrative is that younger British generations are less religious than older ones (Tilley, 2003; Bruce, 2003; Brown 2009; Bagg and Voas, 2009; Davie, 2015, pp. 41–67; Woodhead, 2016). With reference to the Bible, Field notes "the relatively low level of Bible-centricism to be found among the youngest cohort of adults (aged 15–24) and the high level among the over-65s" (2014, p. 518). Rebecca Catto draws on a number of recent studies to argue that indifference is growing amongst British teenagers (2017, pp. 69–72). It could therefore be extrapolated that these young adults are more indifferent towards religion and the Bible than previous generations. Furthermore, if levels of non-religion continue to rise

Table 6.1 A comparison of negative Bible engagement by two non-religious groups

	Not religious and not spiritual	Spiritual but not religious
Feel negative towards the Bible	28%	14%
Disagree that the Bible should be a supreme authority in their lives	87%	45%
Have not engaged with the Bible over the last year	75%	40%
Never see Bible verses on social media	55%	30%
Feel irritated when they see Bible verse on social media	15%	6%
Think it is a negative thing for people to share Bible verses on social media	45%	23%

(Not religious and not spiritual n = 289; spiritual but not religious n = 147).

1 Those who indicated "not applicable" and "don't know" typically responded to the survey as those labelled "not religious and not spiritual". Those who neither affirmed nor rejected the statement responded less negatively but not as positively as the "spiritual but not religious".

indifference towards the Bible will become more widespread and the positive disposition towards it may reduce.

Grace Davie, commenting on the generational decline of religiosity in Britain, also notes that for millennials religion is "very largely an irrelevance in their day to day lives" (2015, p. 88). However, she suggests that they "have lost the rebellious hostility towards formal religion that was characteristic of earlier decades" (p. 88). In other words, she believes that levels of negativity towards religion, and so religious icons like the Bible, are higher amongst baby-boomers and Gen X who have reacted against dominant institutional religious organisations. Thus while these older generations are more familiar with the Bible, they may also be more antagonistic towards it and other aspects of formal religion. It could therefore be that digital millennials are more indifferent but less negative towards the Bible than their parents and grandparents.

Chapter 1 noted that the phrase "Word of God" was popularly associated with the Bible, and Chapter 2 found that there was a greater level of Bible engagement than might be expected. Moreover, some other studies have also found millennials to be more Bible orientated than older generations. For example, Barna's study of Scottish millennials in 2015 found that of all the generations 18 to 24 year-olds were most likely to have a "high" view of the Bible (Barna, 2015, pp. 98–99, 124–125). This adds credence to the claim that millennials have a particular openness to the Bible and other religious or spiritual practices as well. John Micklethwait and Adrian Wooldridge have argued that *God is Back*, and "religion is even (re-)emerging as a force in the very heartland of secularisation [i.e. Europe]" (2009, p. 14). To this way of thinking the positive disposition demonstrated by these young adults is greater than a previous generation and may represent the beginning of a religious resurgence.

The survey, however, provided a snapshot of one cohort of the British population. Further research is required to more clearly capture the place of the Bible in British society. A longitudinal study of one group, such as millennials, and their engagement with the Bible could track any developments over the coming years. An intergenerational study would allow the comparison of different age groups, and repeating the same survey every ten years with British young adults would provide a series of snapshots from which a trajectory could be identified. All three of these options would build upon this study and start to answer some of the questions it has raised.

Indifference: its development

Most digital millennials were indifferent towards the Bible. Religious indifference is something scholars are beginning to explore (Stichweh, 1997; Tonkiss, 2003) and is most recently seen in the edited collection, *Religious Indifference*

(Quack and Schuh, 2017b). Chapter 5 outlined three reasons why indifference among non-Christians was prevalent in Britain compared with a more negative approach in the USA. However, other reasons have been raised as well. It has been suggested that in part it is due to an awareness of how globally diverse humans are and an accompanying belief that tolerance is required for different communities to coexist. It is claimed that in a multicultural modern society, a degree of indifference to religion is required to avoid confrontation. Religion is not the only identifier that must be moderated. Others, perhaps ethnicity or class must be as well (Quack and Schuh, 2017a, p. 9). What is being suggested is that identifiers that separate people should be held more loosely to produce a tolerant and cohesive society.

The promotion of tolerance as a value is important to this argument (Bruce and Voas, 2007) and David Nash points out its role and impact in the current British educational system:

A central part of this has been seeking to engage populations at large with greater knowledge, and apparent understanding, of the religious faiths present in their country. In all aspects of spreading this knowledge, the message of tolerance is uppermost whilst the information is delivered in a deliberately neutral tone.

(Nash, 2017, p. 35)

Bruce and Voas provide further examples of the way in which tolerance towards religions can be seen in British life. They note that speakers are not allowed to criticise other religions on BBC Radio 4's *Thought for the Day* programme, and the religious radio station Premier Christian Radio has been frequently warned by the regulatory body "because its speakers make offensive comments about other religions" (2007, p. 6). There is therefore a live and let live approach to religion in Britain that is built upon tolerance of others and includes an element of indifference, at least in so far as one expresses their views publicly.

While tolerance is promoted, fundamentalism is strongly discouraged. Indeed, the label "fundamentalist" is often used in a derogatory way. Therefore, anyone is held with suspicion who appears to be taking religion too seriously or whose religious views result in behaviour or beliefs that are not affirmed by wider society (Bruce and Voas, 2007, pp. 4–8). This is then another driver towards a more indifferent engagement with and stance towards the Bible.

Nash also highlights that religion in Britain is not only viewed as a private matter, but it is linked to the past and associated with hypocrisy and a moral code that, in part, has been rejected (2017, pp. 36–38). All these factors further reinforce the idea that the Bible is irrelevant and of no use to many nowadays. People may be aware that in the past it played a significant role in the lives of others and continues to in certain parts of the world, but they do not identify a need for it themselves. The Bible, with stories of six-day creation, Jonah and the whale and Jesus walking on water, is dismissed. Indifference is also associated with secularisation (Bruce, 2003). Pierre Bréchon argues that in many European countries the process of secularisation does not lead to the disappearance of religion or the formation of an anti-religious population, but rather to indifference towards religion (2017). A leading scholar who proposes a similar trajectory is David Voas. He and Rodney Ling use data concerning British people's religious identity (or affiliation), belief (in God) and practice to divide the population into three groups. The largest group (36%) they label "fuzzy" and are people who responded positively to two out of the three criteria. The second-largest group (31%) are "unreligious", and they responded negatively to the three criteria. The smallest group are the "religious" (26%), who responded positively to all three (2010). This "fuzzy" group is the one Voas claims will grow over the coming decades and is labelled indifferent (Bagg and Voas, 2009), although it may eventually be overtaken by those who are unreligious (Voas, 2009). To that end, the distribution of digital millennials, with small minorities at both ends and a larger indifferent middle, is along the lines of what would be expected. Sarah Wilkins-Laflamme (2014) suggests that as religion becomes less and less important to more and more people, the degree of indifference will grow. Those who previously identified as nominal or non-practising are more likely to identify as not religious and indifferent, leaving a few marginal, but committed groups who advocate for (and against) religion. In light of this description, it could be argued that British young adults are further down the secularisation road than their American peers (Voas and Chaves, 2016) with a greater swathe of the population being indifferent and minority groups/opinions existing at the edges.

There are therefore many potential and likely factors that have resulted in British digital millennials being indifferent towards the Bible. The weight of influence that should be given to each and their impact upon these young adults is once again something that requires further research. The lived experience of any individual comprises many influences and pressures, and sensitivity is required to unpick the intertwining nature of many of these factors.

Secondary theme: those of other religions were more positive about the Bible than their non-religious peers

It has already been highlighted that a note of caution is required when considering those millennials who identified with a religion other than Christianity, for they are a small group ($n = 267$), and there was evidence that their Bible engagement was not wholly positive. At least half had little or no relationship with the Bible (Table 1.5), and those who had read the Bible in the past year did not always know why they had or what Bible format they used (see Tables 2.4 and 2.8). When asked about the sharing of Bible verses on social media, around a quarter said it was a negative practice (see Figure 3.3). Nonetheless, in general, their stance and engagement was not only greater than non-religious people but was at least comparable with those of non-churchgoing Christians. For example:

- 18% had a positive relationship with the Bible (describing it as exciting or very close), compared with 3% of non-religious people and 9% of non-churchgoers.

- 30% affirmed that the Bible should be a supreme authority in their lives, compared with 6% of non-religious young adults and 19% of non-churchgoers.

- 31% engaged with the Bible at least weekly, compared with 5% of non-religious people and 5% of non-churchgoers.

- 30% saw Bible verses on social media at least weekly, compared with 10% of non-religious people and 12% of non-churchgoers.

- 39% responded positively to seeing Bible verses online, compared with 12% of non-religious people and 37% of non-churchgoers.

Chapter 1 raised some of the possible reasons for this phenomenon, including the possibility that their sense of religious identity has a pluralistic component valuing many religions rather than exclusively their own or that their religion views the Bible as a sacred text. What was not considered was whether Christians view other religious texts positively as well. Table 6.2 presents data exploring how positive a person felt towards the top six religions in Britain and their sacred texts (data that were used in Chapter 1).

While Christians, in general, felt more positive towards the six sacred texts than their non-religious peers did, they were not always as positively disposed to them as those from another religion were. Of all Christians, churchgoers felt most positive towards these other sacred texts and at times their level of response was comparable to those from other religions. This suggests that there may be scope for people of different faiths (and especially those who practice their faith), to use a variety of sacred texts as a basis for discussion and mutual edification. Scriptural reasoning is one such approach. It draws Muslims, Jews and Christians together to read their sacred texts and discuss them (Ford, 2006; Higton, 2009; Higton and Muers, 2012). There is a degree of similarity between the sacred texts of these three Abrahamic faiths, but the data presented here suggest that this approach could be extended to include other religions and their sacred texts as well.

Table 6.2 Positive feelings towards six religions and their sacred texts

	Non-religious	Other religion	Christian		
			All	*Churchgoer*	*Non-churchgoer*
Christianity	20%	42%	70%	80%	60%
Bible	18%	39%	66%	75%	58%
Buddhism	36%	39%	42%	42%	41%
Tripitaka	21%	32%	29%	32%	26%
Hinduism	21%	33%	32%	33%	30%
Vedas	14%	34%	25%	29%	21%
Judaism	15%	29%	31%	38%	24%
Torah	13%	35%	31%	40%	23%
Sikhism	19%	32%	26%	31%	22%
Guru Granth Sahib	12%	32%	25%	32%	18%
Islam	12%	45%	22%	28%	17%
Qur'an	10%	46%	21%	27%	16%

(*n* = 1,879 with the "Churchgoer" and "Non-churchgoer" being represented in the "All" category as well).

It also suggests that there is a common appreciation across religions of each other's sacred text(s) and faith. Among Christians, this again is more strongly seen amongst churchgoers, in other words, practitioners. If this is also the case for other religious millennials, then it starts to counter the popular argument, highlighted earlier, that taking religion seriously is dangerous. In this instance, those Christian young adults who practised their faith (i.e. churchgoers) felt most positive towards other religions and their sacred texts compared with non-religious people or non-churchgoing Christians. This would indicate that indifference or the holding lightly of religious identity and practice is not the only way to achieve social cohesion. Indeed, it may not be the best way of drawing different people groups together to form one society.

Secondary theme: women were not more religious than men

Chapters 1–3 also found that millennial women were not more Bible orientated than men. For example:

- 10% of women had an exciting or very close relationship with the Bible but so did 14% of men.
- 18% of women agreed with the statement that the Bible should be a supreme authority in their life but so did 23% of men.
- 15% of women engaged at least weekly with the Bible but so did 24% of men.

- 17% of women saw Bible verses weekly on social media but so did 24% of men.
- 29% of women responded positively to seeing a Bible verse on social media but so did 34% of men.

This was not always the case. In a few instances, women were more positive about the Bible than men, for example:

- 40% of women felt positive towards the Bible and 14% felt negative towards it, while 37% of men felt positive towards it and 18% felt negative towards it.
- 44% of women agree that it is a positive thing to share Bible verses on social media, compared with 38% of men.

These though were a minority of cases. When other data from the survey was examined women were consistently found not to be more religiously orientated than their male peers. They were more likely to identify as not religious (52%) than the men (44%), as likely to identify as Christian (34% women, 36% men) and less likely to attend church regularly (20% women, 32% men). This was similarly the case with the women from the Bible-centric cohort, who were not more Bible orientated than their male peers either. Therefore, while it would be expected that female digital millennials would be more religiously inclined than men, and Field's meta-analysis of Bible survey data concluded that "on all measures women are more Bible-centric than men" (2014, p. 518), this was not the case.

This finding challenges some theories that attempt to explain the religious gender difference. For instance, some have claimed that the higher religiosity of women is due to their biological makeup resulting in them being more risk-averse and so more likely to practise a religion and less likely to identify as not religious (Stark, 2002). On the understanding that there is no unique biological phenomenon that would cause 18 to 35 year old women to become less risk-averse, this theory is found wanting. The data do correspond with theories claiming that secularisation impacted men initially more than women, and that is why women have been less religious. It could therefore be that millennial women have caught up with their male peers and are now as secular (Trzebiatowska and Bruce, 2012). It also fits with claims that women are more religious because they are often more deeply involved in key life moments that some view as sacred, such as giving birth or caring for elderly dying parents (Davie, 2007). Therefore, for young women who are less likely to have children or be caring for elderly parents, religion may play less of a role. Indeed the survey data showed that young mothers were more religious and Bible orientated than those adults

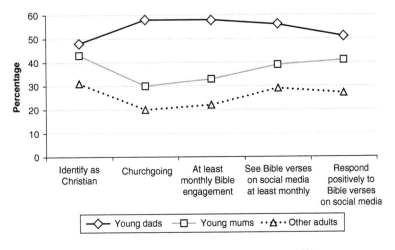

Figure 6.1 Young dads' and young mums' religiosity (*n* = 1, 943).

who had no children (see Figure 6.1). What stands out, however, is that young dads were even more religious than young mums.

There are other theories that attempt to explain the religious gender difference (de Vaus and McAllister, 1987; Voas, McAndrew and Storm, 2013; Schmitt *et al.*, 2017), and further research is required to capture the nature of this unexpected finding and its implication for how religiosity is understood in Britain. What can be concluded at this stage is that theories for religious gender difference that emphasise the role of nature (i.e. biological reason) are less likely to be affirmed by the data than theories that focus on nurture (i.e. societal and cultural reasons).

Additionally, among these digital millennials, women were slightly more likely to engage with paper/traditional formats than men:

- 62% of women normally read from a paper book, and 16% used a digital device. This compares with 54% of men who read from a paper book and 20% who normally used a digital device.
- 50% of women preferred the image of the paper Bible, 24% preferred the image of the digital one, and 43% of men preferred the paper Bible, and 31% the image of the digital one.
- The top three Bible formats used by women were: don't know (26%); read from a paper Bible (25%); and read using a digital platform (14%). For men however digital came first: Search the Bible using a digital platform (23%); read using a digital platform (22%) and read from a paper Bible (20%).

Therefore, although the earlier data demonstrated that women were not more religious than men, they continue to be drawn to more traditional forms of (Bible) reading technology, even though these are young adults who have been part of the digital revolution. Whatever changes in society have resulted in a reframing of the role of gender and religiosity, they have not had a similar effect upon the role of gender and technology.

Secondary theme: digital Bible technology does not dominate digital millennials

Finally, Chapters 1–3 also demonstrated that digital millennials are not as digitally orientated as might be expected. For example:

- They preferred the image of the paper Bible (47%) to the digital one (28%) (26% were drawn to neither).
- 58% normally read from a paper book and 18% from a digital book (24% used both equally).
- Of those who had engaged with the Bible in the past year, the top Bible format they used was reading from a paper Bible (22%). This was closely followed, though, by don't know (19%), reading using a digital device (19%), searching the Bible using a digital device (18%) and listening to someone else read the Bible (14%).
- 48% never or very infrequently see Bible verses shared on social media.
- 51% of those who do see Bible verses find them irrelevant.

Digital (Bible) reading technology has not overtaken traditional technologies. This was especially true for the Bible-centric group presented in Chapter 4 for they strongly preferred the image of the paper Bible (71%) and normally read from a paper book (72%). The top Bible formats they use were reading a paper Bible (57%), reading using a digital device (20%) and listening to someone else read the Bible (16%). While they do see Bible verses on social media very regularly, 85% doing so at least weekly, they are unlikely to post Bible verses themselves (7% doing so at least weekly).

These young adults grew up in a digital age, one marked by the popularity of the personal computer and the advent of social media. They were part of the digital revolution brought about by the World Wide Web, which was then made personal through the development of smartphones. Bible agencies, churches and parachurch organisations have invested heavily in the production of thousands of digital Bible resources. These and other digital innovations are used, many on a daily basis, by this section of society, yet their engagement with the Bible is still orientated towards older technology. They have not rejected digital Bible technology nor wholeheartedly embraced it at the expense of more traditional Bible formats; at present both technologies are coexisting.

The preference for paper Bibles will be a conscious choice for some of these young adults. There are features common to most books and it may be that there is a greater receptivity to books in general, which spills over to impact the Bible, as discussed in Chapter 1. The physicality of the Bible itself could be important to them. The paper book is a physical object upon which a myriad of different attributes, feelings, expectations, memories, desires and significance can be placed. In the West, paper Bibles have a classic feel, often bound in leather with a two-column layout and printed on very thin paper. Therefore, when accessing a Bible passage on a smartphone or tablet, with its multipurpose nature and lack of classical Bible features, those attributes and feelings associated with the Bible may be lost or diminished. It may also be that digital millennials are aware of some of the limits of digital Bible technology. Smartphone screens are not always easy to read and they show only a small section of the Bible often isolated from its surrounding context. They also lend to a more superficial reading style and can be accompanied by distracting adverts and interruptions. Paper technology can lend itself to a longer and more engaging reading of the Bible (Liu, 2008; Weaver, 2017; Siker, 2017, pp. 57–96).

It could also be that the Bible format used is one they typically have little choice over. For instance, if they are engaging with the Bible in a special church service then the person leading the service will have decided what format to use from the pulpit, and the church may (or may not) hand out paper Bibles as people walk into the service. Receiving a Bible as a gift is still a relatively common practice and may occur in a church setting or at a school assembly. Once again though, the Bible that is given is a paper Bible.

Of course, digital Bibles are a very recent phenomenon and their use may continue to increase over the coming years. In light of digital millennials' preference for paper Bibles and the way technologies have developed in the past, it is perhaps unlikely that paper Bibles will disappear. Twenty years ago, Ilana Snyder reflected on the role of changing technologies and wrote:

> Even though printing completely replaced handwriting in book production, it did not spell the end for handwriting. Rather, the boundaries between the two writing technologies blurred. Today pen and paper serve for notes and personal communications; word processing and typewriting are for texts not ready—or appropriate—for typesetting. The future

of writing is not a linear progression in which new technologies usurp earlier ones. A more likely scenario is that a number of technologies will continue to co-exist, interact, even complement each other.

(1998, p. xxi)

In the coming years, digital and paper Bibles may therefore coexist fulfilling different roles in the various contexts in which they are engaged.

Conclusion

This study has provided a snapshot showing the place of the Bible in the lives of one cohort of British society: digital millennials. In terms of their stance towards the Bible, use of it and how it is engaged with on social media, most young adults are indifferent towards it. Many feel neither positive nor negative towards the Bible (40%); rarely make use of it (61%) and ignore or never see Bible verses on social media (53%). There is a minority, however, who are more positively disposed towards and engaged with the Bible. They feel positive towards it (38%); use it weekly (20%) and feel inspired, encouraged or comforted when they see Bible verses on social media (32%). There is an even smaller group as well who are more negatively disposed. They feel negative towards the Bible (16%); are irritated or uncomfortable when they see Bible verses on social media (13%) and think it is a negative thing to share Bible verses online (24%).

The indifference noted among the majority is also seen in how few Bible-centric Christians post Bible verses online, for there is little point in communicating something widely that is of little interest to their peers. It is also highlighted when data from Britain and the USA are compared, especially when exploring how non-Christians regard the Bible. In Britain, they are generally indifference towards it, while in the USA they are more antagonistic. In Britain, therefore, the Bible is treated with a qualified indifference by digital millennials.

References

American Bible Society. (2017). *State of the Bible 2017*. Retrieved from https://1s712. americanbible.org/cdn-www-ws03/uploads/content/State_of_the_Bible_2017_ report_032317.pdf

———. (2018). *State of the Bible 2018*. Retrieved from https://1s712.americanbible. org/cdn-www-ws03/uploads/content/State_of_the_Bible_2018_Report_-_Han_ Solo.pdf

Bagg, S. and Voas, D. (2009). The Triumph of Indifference: Irreligion in British Society. In P. Zuckerman (Ed.), *Atheism and Secularity: Volume 2: Global Expressions* (pp. 91–111). Santa Barbara, CA: Praeger.

Barna. (2014, October 21). Millennials and the Bible: 3 Surprising Insights [Blog post]. Retrieved from https://www.barna.com/research/millennials-and-the-bible-3-surprising-insights/

———. (2015). *Transforming Scotland*. Ventura, CA: Barna Group.

———. (2016). *The Bible in America*. Ventura, CA: Barna Group.

———. (2018). *Spiritual Conversations in the Digital Age*. Ventura, CA: Barna Group.

Barna, American Bible Society and InterVarsity Christian Fellowship. (2014). *Millennials and the Bible 2014*. Retrieved from https://1s712.americanbible. org/cdn-www-ws03/uploads/content/Millennials_and_the_Bible_Report_ %28Barna%2C_ABS__InterVarsity%29.pdf

BBC. (2017, April 9). Resurrection did not happen, say quarter of Christians. BBC news. Retrieved from https://www.bbc.co.uk/news/uk-england-39153121

Beal, T. (2011). *The Rise and Fall of the Bible: The Unexpected History of an Accidental Book*. New York: Mariner Books.

Bebbington, D. W. (1989). *Evangelicalism in Modern Britain: A History from the 1730s to the 1980s*. London: Unwin Hyman.

Bellar, W., Campbell, H. A., Cho, K. J., Terry, A., Tsuria, R., Yadlin-Segal, A. and Ziemer, J. (2013). Reading Religion in Internet Memes. *Journal of Religion, Media and Digital Culture*, 2(2), 1–39.

Bennett, S., Maton, K. and Kervin, L. (2008). The 'Digital Natives' Debate: A Critical Review of the Evidence. *British Journal of Educational Technology*, 39(5), 775–786.

Berger, P., Davie, G. and Fokas, E. (2008). *Religious America, Secular Europe? A Theme and Variations*. Farnham, United Kingdom: Ashgate.

Bibb, B. (2017). Readers and Their e-Bibles: The Shape and Authority of the Hypertext Canon. In P. Goff, A. E. Farnsley II and P. J. Thusesen (Eds.), *The Bible in American Life* (pp. 256–265). New York: OUP.

Bible Society. (2014). *Pass it On*. Retrieved from http://www.biblesociety.org.uk/press/uploads/final-copy-of-Pass-it-On-research-report_02070706.pdf

———. (2016). *You and Your Bible*. Retrieved from https://www.biblesociety.org.uk/content/get_involved/you_and_your_bible/you_and_your_bible_report.pdf

Bielo, J. S. (2009). *Words Upon the Word: An Ethnography of Evangelical Group Bible Study*. New York: New York University Press.

Blyth, C. (2015). Lisbeth and Leviticus: Biblical Literacy and *The Girl with the Dragon Tattoo*. In K. B. Edwards (Ed.), *Rethinking Biblical Literacies* (pp. 165–185). London: Bloomsbury.

Bréchon, P. (2017). Measuring Religious Indifference in International Sociological Quantitative Surveys (EVS and ISSP). In J. Quack and C. Schuh (Eds.), *Religious Indifference: New Perspectives from Studies on Secularization and Nonreligion* (pp. 143–170). Cham, Switzerland: Springer.

Brierley, P. (2006). *Pulling out of the Nose Dive: A Contemporary Picture of Churchgoing*. London: Christian Research.

———. (2013). *Capital Growth: The London Church Census*. Tonbridge, United Kingdom: ADBC Publishers.

Brown, C. (2009 [2001]). *The Death of Christian Britain: Understanding Secularisation 1800–2000*. (2nd ed.). Abingdon, United Kingdom: Routledge.

Bruce, S. (2003). The Demise of Christianity in Britain. In G. David, P. Heelas and L. Woodhead (Eds.), *Predicting Religion: Christian, Secular and Alternative Futures* (pp. 53–63). Aldershot, United Kingdom: Ashgate.

Bruce S. and Voas, D. (2007). Religious Toleration and Organisational Typologies. *Journal of Contemporary Religion*, 22(1), 1–17.

Bury, L. (2013, November 25). Young Adult Readers "Prefer Printed to ebooks". *The Guardian*. Retrieved from https://www.theguardian.com/books/2013/nov/25/young-adult-readers-prefer-printed-ebooks

Campbell, L. (2018, July 19). British publishing breaks revenue records but textbook sales are hit. *The Bookseller*. Retrieved from https://www.thebookseller.com/news/british-publishing-houses-break-all-revenue-records-textbook-sales-take-hit-833321

Catto, R. (2017). Interfaith Dialogue and the Challenge of Indifference. In J. Quack and C. Schuh (Eds.), *Religious Indifference: New Perspectives from Studies on Secularization and Nonreligion* (pp. 65–82). Cham, Switzerland: Springer.

Cheong, P. (2014). Tweet the Message? Religious Authority and Social Media Innovation. *Journal of Religion, Media and Digital Culture*, 3(3), 1–19.

Clivaz, C. (2014). New Testament in a Digital Culture: A *Biblaridion* (little book) lost in the web? *Journal of Religion, Media and Digital Culture*, 3(3), 20–38.

Cole, A. and Ovwigho, P. C. (2012). *Bible Engagement as the Key to Spiritual Growth: A Research Synthesis*. USA: The Good News Broadcasting Association.

Collins, M. A. (2015). Loss of the Bible and the Bible in *Lost*: Biblical Literacy and Mainstream Television. In K. B. Edwards (Ed.), *Rethinking Biblical Literacies* (pp. 71–94). London: Bloomsbury.

ComRes. (2011). *The Influence of the Bible*. Retrieved from http://www.comresglo bal.com/wp-content/themes/comres/poll/Bible_Society_Tables_April_2011.pdf

———. (2017). *Church Mapping Survey*. Retrieved from http://www.comresglobal. com/wp-content/uploads/2017/09/Church-of-England-Church-Mapping-Survey-Data-Tables.pdf

Crossley, J. G. (2011). Biblical Literacy and the English King James Liberal Bible: A Twenty-First Century Tale of Capitalism, Nationalism and Nostalgia. *Postscripts*, 7(2), 197–211.

———. (2016a). *Harnessing Chaos: The Bible in English Political Discourse since 1968*. London: Bloomsbury.

———. (2016b). Brexit Barrow: Real-Time Receptions of the Bible during a Summer of Political Chaos, *Relegere*, 6(1), 19–60.

Crystal, D. (2010). *Begat: The King James Bible and the English Language*. Oxford, United Kingdom: OUP.

Davie, G. (2002). *Europe: The Exceptional Case, Parameters of Faith in the Modern World*. London: Darton, Longman and Todd.

———. (2007). Vicarious Religion: A Methodological Challenge. In N. T. Ammerman (Ed.), *Everyday Religion: Observing Modern Religious Lives* (pp. 21–35). Oxford, United Kingdom: OUP.

———. (2015). *Religion in Britain: A Persistent Paradox*. Chichester, United Kingdom: John Wiley and Sons.

De Certeau, M. (1984). *The Practice of Everyday Life*. Trans. S. F. Rendall. Berkeley, CA: University of California.

De Vaus, D. and McAllister, I. (1987). Gender Difference in Religion: A Test of the Structural Location Theory. *American Sociological Review*, 52(4), 472–481.

Drescher, E. and Anderson, K. (2012). *Click 2 Save: The Digital Ministry Bible*. Harrisburg, PA: Morehouse.

Edwards, K. B. (2012). *Admen and Eve: The Bible in Contemporary Advertising*. Sheffield, United Kingdom: Sheffield Phoenix Press.

———. (2015). *Rethinking Biblical Literacy*. London: Bloomsbury.

Evangelical Alliance. (2014). *Time for Discipleship?* London: Evangelical Alliance.

———. (2015). *Building Tomorrow's Church Today*. London: Evangelical Alliance.

———. (2016). *Talking Jesus: Perceptions of Jesus, Christians and Evangelism in England*. London: Evangelical Alliance.

Field, C. D. (2014). Is the Bible Becoming a Closed Book? British opinion Poll Evidence. *Journal of Contemporary Religion*, 29(3), 503–528.

Folio Society Survey. (2014, November 18). The Most Influential Books of the Moment (Blog post). Retrieved from https://blogs.foliosociety.com/the-most-influential-books-of-the-moment/

Ford, D. F. (2006). An Interfaith Wisdom: Scriptural Reasoning Between Jews, Christians and Muslims. *Modern Theology*, 22(3), 345–366.

Ford, D. G. (2018). *Reading the Bible Outside the Church: A Case Study*. Eugene, OR: Pickwick Publications.

Foster, S. (2016). *What Helps Disciples Grow? Saltley Trust Faith and Learning Series 2*. Retrieved from http://www.saltleytrust.org.uk/wpcontent/%0Duploads/delightful-downloads/2016/04/What-Helps-Disciples-%0DGrow.pdf

Genette, G. (1997). *Paratexts: Thresholds of Interpretation*. Cambridge, United Kingdom: CUP.

Giles, D. (2016). *Putting Your Faith in Social Media: How are Faith-Sharing Activities Facilitated and Enabled in a Social Media Age?* (Unpublished master's dissertation) University for the Creative Arts (Farnham), United Kingdom. Retrieved from https://issuu.com/salvationarmyihq/docs/putting_your_faith_in_social_media_

Giorgio, F. (2016, September 22). Facebook Retains Social Media Crown for UK Millennials (Blog post). Retrieved from https://www.comscore.com/Insights/Data-Mine/Facebook-retains-Social-Media-crown-for-UK-Millennials

Goff, P., Farnsley II, A. E. and Thuesen, P. J. (Eds.), (2017). *The Bible in American Life*. New York: OUP.

Gould, M. (2015). *The Social Media Gospel: Sharing the Good News in New Ways*. Collegeville, MN: Liturgical Press.

Guest, M., Aune, K., Sharma, S. and Warner, R. (2013). *Christianity and the University Experience*. London: Bloomsbury.

Helsper, E. and Enyon, R. (2009). Digital Natives: where is the evidence? *British Educational Research Journal*, 36(3), 1–18.

Hewitt, B. and R. Powys-Smith, C. (2011a). *Bible Engagement in England and Wales*. United Kingdom: Bible Society and Christian Research.

———. (2011b). *Data Tables for Bible Engagement in England and Wales*. United Kingdom: Bible Society and Christian Research.

Hiemstra, R. (2014). *Confidence, Conversation and Community: Bible Engagement in Canada, 2013*. Toronto, Canada: Faith Today Publications.

Higton, M. (2009). Scriptural Reasoning. *Conversations in Religion and Theology*, 7(2), 129–133.

Higton, M. and Muers, R. (2012). *The TEXT in PLAY: Experiments in Reading Scripture*. Eugene, OR: Cascade.

Hooker, A. W. (2015). Mary, Mary, Quite Contrary: Eve as Redemptrix in Madonna's "Girl Gone Wild". In K. B. Edwards (Ed.), *Rethinking Biblical Literacy* (pp. 119–142). London: Bloomsbury.

Hout, M. and Fishers, C. (2014). Explaining Why More Americans Have No Religious Preference: Political Backlash and Generational Succession, 1987–2012. *Sociological Science*, 1, 423–47.

Howe, N. and Strauss, W. (2000). *Millennials Rising: The Next Great Generation*. New York: Vintage.

Hughes P. and Pickering, C. (2010). *Bible Engagement among Young Australians: Patterns and Social Drivers*. Australia: Christian Research Association.

Hutchings, T. (2015a). E-Reading and the Christian Bible. *Studies in Religion/Sciences Religieuses*, 44(4), 423–440.

———. (2015b). "The Smartest Way to Study the Word": Protestant and Catholic Approaches to the Digital Bible. In M. D. Bosch, J. L. Micó and J. M. Carbonell (Eds.), *Negotiating Religious Visibility in Digital Media* (pp. 57–68). Barcelona, Spain: Blanquerna Observatory on Media, Religion and Culture.

IPSOS MORI. (2001, January 14). *Divine Inspiration is Our Speciality.* Retrieved from https://www.ipsos.com/ipsos-mori/en-uk/divine-inspiration-our-speciality

Johnson, T. M., Zurlo, G. A., Hickman, A. W. and Crossing, P. F. (2016). Christianity 2016: Latin America and Projecting Religions to 2050. *International Bulletin of Mission Research*, 40(1), 22–29.

Kinnaman, D. (2007). *unChristian: What A New Generation Really Thinks About Christianity ... And Why it Matters.* Grand Rapids, MI: Baker Books.

Knott, K., Poole, E. and Taira, T. (n.d.). Media Coverage of Religion is Up, Even Though Traditional Religious Practice is Down, *Religion and Society.* Retrieved from http://www.religionandsociety.org.uk/uploads/docs/2011_03/1301305944_Knott_Phase_1_Large_Grant_Block.pdf

Kukulska-Hulme, A. (2008). Human Factors and Innovation with Mobile Devices. In T. Hansson (Ed.), *Handbook of Research on Digital Information Technologies: Innovations, Methods, and Ethical Issues* (pp. 387–397). Hershey, PA: Information Science Reference.

Le Grys, A. (2010). *Shaped by God's Story: Making Sense of the Bible.* London: Lulu Publishing.

Lee, L. (2014). Secular or Nonreligious? Investigating and Interpreting Generic "Not Religious" Categories and Populations. *Religion*, 44(3), 466–482.

Lee, M. (2016, May 20). Scripture as Spam: What 5 Experts Think About Twitter Bible Bots. *Christianity Today.* Retrieved from http://www.christianitytoday.com/ct/2016/june/spamming-good-news-twitter-bots-more-bible-verses-pastors.html?start=1

LifeWay Research. (2017). *American Views on Bible Reading.* Retrieved from http://lifewayresearch.com/wp-content/uploads/2017/04/Sept-2016-American-Views-Bible-Reading.pdf

Liu, Z. (2008). *Paper to Digital: Documents in the Information Age.* Westport, CT: Libraries Unlimited.

Malley, B. (2004). *How the Bible Works: An Anthropological Study of Evangelical Biblicism.* Walnut Creek, CA: Altamira Press.

Mann. J. L. (2017). Reflections on the Church of England's Daily Prayer App. *Heidelberg Journal of Religions on the Internet*, 12, 42–59.

———. (2018). How Technology Means: Texts, Histories, and their Associated Technologies. *Digital Humanities Quarterly*, 12(3), n.p.

———. (forthcoming). *Computing the Bible: A Brief History.* London, United Kingdom: Routledge.

Mark, O. (2016). *Passing on Faith.* London: Theos.

Meredith, C. (2015). A Big Room for Poo: Eddie Izzard's Bible and the Literacy of Laughter. In K. B. Edwards (Ed.), *Rethinking Biblical Literacy* (pp. 187–212), London: Bloomsbury.

Micklethwait, J. and Wooldridge, A. (2009). *God is Back: How the Global Rise of Faith is Changing the World*. New York: Allen Lane.

Mohler, A. (2016, January 20). The Scandal of Biblical Illiteracy: It's Our Problem (Blog post). Retrieved from https://albertmohler.com/2016/01/20/the-scandal-of-biblical-illiteracy-its-our-problem-4/)

Momentum, (2009). *Young Adult Survey*. United Kingdom: Momentum.

Morgan G. and Idriss, S. (2012). "Corsages on their Parents' Jackets": Employment and Aspiration Among Arabic-Speaking Youth in Western Sydney. *Journal of Youth Studies*, 15(7), 929–943.

Myles, R. J. (2015). Biblical Literacy and *The Simpsons*. In K. B. Edwards (Ed.). *Rethinking Biblical Literacy* (pp. 143–164). London: Bloomsbury.

Nash, D. (2017). Genealogies of Indifference? New Theoretical Thoughts on the History and Creation of Narratives Surrounding Christianity, Secularism and Indifference. In J. Quack and C. Schuh (Eds.), *Religious Indifference: New Perspectives from Studies on Secularization and Nonreligion* (pp. 25–42). Cham, Switzerland: Springer.

Noll, M. A. (2017). The Bible: Then and Now. In P. Goff, A. E. Farnsley II and P. J. Thuesen (Eds.). *The Bible in American Life* (pp. 331–344). New York: OUP.

Perrin, R. H. (2016). *The Bible Reading of Young Evangelicals: An Exploration of the Ordinary Hermeneutics and Faith of Generation Y*. Eugene, OR: Pickwick Publications.

Phillips, P. M. (2017). *Engaging the Word: Biblical Literacy and Christian Discipleship*. Abingdon, United Kingdom: Bible Reading Fellowship.

———. (2018). The Pixelated Text: Reading the Bible within Digital Culture. *Theology*, 121(6), 403–412.

———. (forthcoming). *The Bible, Social Media and Digital Culture*. London: Routledge.

Pietersen, L. (2011). *Reading the Bible after Christendom*. Harrisonburg, VA: Herald Press.

Prensky, M. (2001a). Digital Natives, Digital Immigrants: Part 1. *On the Horizon*, 9(5), 1–6.

———. (2001b). Digital Natives, Digital immigrants: Part 2: Do They Really Think Differently? *On the Horizon*, 9(6), 1–6.

Quack, J. and Schuh, C. (2017a). Conceptualising Religious Indifferences in Relation to Religion and Nonreligion. In J. Quack and C. Schuh (Eds.), *Religious Indifference: New Perspectives from Studies on Secularization and Nonreligion* (pp. 1–23). Cham, Switzerland: Springer.

———. (Eds.), (2017b). *Religious Indifference: New Perspectives from Studies on Secularization and Nonreligion*. Cham, Switzerland: Springer.

Rafoss, T. W. (2017). *Nordmenns Bibelbruk*. Olso, Norway: Institutt for kirke-, religions- og livssynsforstning. Retrieved from: http://www.kifo.no/wp-content/uploads/2017/05/KIFO-Rapport-2017_1_Nordmenns-bibelbruk-m-omslag.pdf

Rainer, T. S. and Rainer, J. W. (2011). *Millennials: Connecting to America's Largest Generation*. Nashville, TN: B&H.

Reed, E. D., Freathy, R., Cornwall, S. and Davis, A. (2013). Narrative Theology in Religious Education. *British Journal of Religious Education*, 35(3), 297–312.

Rogers, A. P. (2015). *Congregational Hermeneutics: How Do We Read?* Farnham, United Kingdom: Ashgate.

Rosenblatt, L. M. (1995 [1965]). *Literature as Exploration*. New York: Modern Language Association of America.

Rudgard, O. (2017, September 14). Most Church of England Christians Never Read the Bible, Survey finds. *The Telegraph*. Retrieved from https://www.telegraph.co.uk/news/2017/09/14/church-england-christians-never-read-bible-survey-finds/

Schmitt, D. P., Long, A. E., McPhearson, A., O"Brien, K., Remmert, B. and Shah, S. H. (2017). Personality and gender differences in global perspective. *International Journal of Psychology*, 52(S1) 45–56.

Schnabel, L. and Bock, S. (2017). The Persistent and Exceptional Intensity of American Religion: A Response to Recent Research. *Sociological Science*, 4: 686–700.

Sherwood, Y. (2000). *A Biblical Text and Its Afterlives: The Survival of Jonah in Western Culture*. Cambridge, United Kingdom: CUP.

———. (2012). *Biblical Blaspheming: Trials of the Sacred for a Secular Age*. Cambridge, United Kingdom: CUP.

Siker, J. S. (2017). *Liquid Scripture: The Bible in a Digital World*. Minneapolis, MN: Fortress Press.

Smietana, B. (2017, April 25). LifeWay Research: Americans Are Fond of the Bible, Don't Actually Read it. Retrieved from https://lifewayresearch.com/2017/04/25/lifeway-research-americans-are-fond-of-the-bible-dont-actually-read-it/

Smith, B. (2013, November 25). 62% of 16–24s Prefer Books as Physical Products (Blog post). *Voxburner*. Retrieved from http://www.voxburner.com/blog-source/2015/5/18/16-24-prefer-books-as-physical-products?rq=ebooks

Snyder, I. (1998). "Page to Screen" in I. Snyder (Ed.), *Page to Screen: Taking Literacy into the Electronic Era* (pp. xx–xxxvi). London: Routledge.

Spencer, N. (2005). *Beyond the Fringe: Researching a Spiritual Age*. Hope Valley, United Kingdom: Cliff College Publishing.

Stark, R. (2002). Physiology and Faith: Addressing the "Universal" Gender Difference in Religious Commitment. *Journal for the Scientific Study of Religion*, 41(3), 465–507.

Statistica (2017). *Main Social Networking Site Preference in the United Kingdom (UK) 2016, by Age*. Retrieved from https://www.statista.com/statistics/308712/main-social-networking-site-preference-in-the-uk-by-age/

———. (2018a). *Penetration of Leading Social Networks in India as of 3rd Quarter 2017*. Retrieved from https://www.statista.com/statistics/284436/india-social-network-penetration/

———. (2018b). *Penetration of Leading Social Networks in Saudi Arabia as of 3rd Quarter 2017*. Retrieved from https://www.statista.com/statistics/284451/saudi-arabia-social-network-penetration/

Stetzer, E. (2015, July 6). The Epidemic of Bible Illiteracy in Our Churches. *Christianity Today*. Retrieved from https://www.christianitytoday.com/edstetzer/2015/july/epidemic-of-bible-illiteracy-in-our-churches.html

Stichweh, R. (1997). The Stranger—On the Sociology of the Indifference. *Thesis Eleven*, 51(1), 1–16.

Tapscott, D. (1998). *Growing up Digital: The Rise of the Net Generation.* New York: McGraw-Hill.

Taylor, B. (2016). *Sharing Faith Using Social Media.* Cambridge, United Kingdom: Grove Books.

Taylor, P. (2014). *The Next America: Boomers, Millennials, and the Looming Generational Showdown.* Philadelphia, PA: PublicAffairs.

Theos. (2012). *Post-Religious Britain: The Faith of the Faithless.* London: Theos.

Tilley, J. R. (2003). Secularization and Aging in Britain: Does Family Formation Cause Greater Religiosity? *Journal for the Scientific Study of Religion*, 42(2), 269–278.

Tonkiss, F. (2003). The Ethics of Indifference: Community and Solitude in the City. *International Journal of Cultural Studies*, 6(3), 297–311.

Trzebiatowska, M. and Bruce, S. (2012). *Why Are Women More Religious Than Men?* Oxford, United Kingdom: OUP.

Twenge, J. M. (2014). *Generation Me: Why Today's Young Americans are More Confident, Assertive, Entitled—and More Miserable than Ever Before.* (2nd ed.). New York: Atria.

Underwood, J. (2007). Rethinking the Digital Divide: Impacts on Student Tutor Relationships. *European Journal of Education*, 42(2), 213–222.

Voas. D. (2009). The Rise and Fall of Fuzzy Fidelity in Europe. *European Sociological Review*, 25(2), 155–168.

Voas D. and Chaves, M. (2016). Is the United States a Counterexample to the Secularization Thesis? *American Journal of Sociology*, 121(5), 1517–1556.

Voas, D. and Ling, R. (2010). Religion in Britain and the United States. In A. Park, J. Curtis, K. Thomson, M. Phillips, E. Clery and S. Butt (Eds). *British Social Attitudes: the 26th Report* (pp. 65–86). London: SAGE.

Voas, D., McAndrew, S. and Storm, I. (2013). Modernisation and the Gender Gap in Religiosity: Evidence from Cross-National European Surveys. *KZfSS Kölner Zeitschrift für Soziologie und Sozialpsychologie*, 65(1), 259–283.

Voas, D. and Storm, I. (2012). The Intergenerational Transmission of Churchgoing in England and Australia. *Review of Religious Research*, 53, 377–395

Weaver, J. B. (2017). American Bible Reading in Digital Culture. In P. Goff, A. E. Farnsley II and P. J. Thusesen (Eds.). *The Bible in American Life* (pp. 249–255), New York: OUP.

Wilkins-Laflamme, S. (2014). Towards Religious Polarization? Time Effects on Religious Commitment in US, UK and Canadian Regions. *Sociology of Religion*, 75(2), 284–308.

Woodhead, L. (2016). The Rise of "No Religion" in Britain: The Emergence of a New Cultural Majority. *Journal of the British Academy*, 4, 245–261.

Index

For Product Safety Concerns and Information please contact our EU
representative GPSR@taylorandfrancis.com
Taylor & Francis Verlag GmbH, Kaufingerstraße 24, 80331 München, Germany

www.ingramcontent.com/pod-product-compliance
Ingram Content Group UK Ltd.
Pitfield, Milton Keynes, MK11 3LW, UK
UKHW021423080625
459435UK00011B/129